POE S

BY

LYDIA H. SIGOURNEY

H. Corbould pinx.^{t} Davenport sculp.^{t}

The Disappointed

POEMS

BY

LYDIA H. SIGOURNEY

NEW YORK:
LEAVITT & ALLEN BROS.,
No. 8 HOWARD STREET.

CONTENTS.

POEMS

BY

LYDIA H. SIGOURNEY.

THE FIRST MORNING OF SPRING.

Break from your chains, ye lingering streams
Rise, blossoms, from your wintry dreams;
Drear fields, your robes of verdure take;
Birds, from your trance of silence wake;
Glad trees, resume your leafy crown;
Shrubs, o'er the mirror-brooks bend down;
Bland zephyrs, wheresoe'er ye stray,
The Spring doth call you,—come away.
Thou too, my soul, with quicken'd force
Pursue thy brief, thy measur'd course;

With grateful zeal each power employ;
Catch vigour from Creation's joy;
And deeply on thy shortening span
Stamp *love to God and love to man.*

But Spring, with tardy step, appears,
Chill is her eye, and moist with tears;
Still are the founts in fetters bound,—
The flower-germs shrink within the ground.
Where are the warblers of the sky?
I ask,—and angry blasts reply.
It is not thus in heavenly bowers.—
Nor ice-bound rill, nor drooping flowers,
Nor silent harp, nor folded wing,
Invade that everlasting Spring
Toward which we look with wishful tear,
While pilgrims in this wintry sphere.

"NOT DEAD, BUT SLEEPETH."

Not dead? A marble seal is prest,
  Where her bright glance did part,
A weight is on the pulseless breast,
  And ice around the heart;
No more she wakes with greeting smile,
  Gay voice, and buoyant tread,
But yet ye calmly say the while,
  She sleeps, she is not dead.

If thou dost mourn for ashes cold,—
  A voice from heaven replied,
" Then be thine anguish uncontroll'd,
  Thy tears a heathen tide;
Thine idol was that vestment fair
  Which wraps the spirit free,
Earth, air, and water, claim their share,
  Say! which shall comfort thee?

But the strong mind whose heaven-born thought
  No earthly chain could bind,

The holy heart divinely fraught
  With love to all mankind,
The humble soul whose early trust
  Was with its God on high,
These were thy sister, who in dust
  May *sleep*, but cannot *die*."

THE COMMUNION.

"Master! it is good to be here."
MARK, ix. 5

THEY knelt them side by side; the hoary man
Whose memory was an age, and she whose cheek
Gleam'd like that velvet which the young moss rose
Puts blushing forth from its scarce sever'd sheath.
There was the sage,—whose eye of science spans
The comet in his path of fire,—and she
Whose household duty was her sole delight
And highest study. On the chancel clasp'd,
In meek devotion, were those bounteous hands
Which pour forth charities, unask'd, untir'd,—
And his which roughly win the scanty bread

For his young children. There the man of might
On bended knee, fast by his servant's side,
Sought the same Master,—brethren in one faith.
And fellow-pilgrims.
See yon wrinkled brow,
Where care and grief for many a year have trac'd
Alternate furrows,—bow'd so near those lips,
Which but the honey and the dew of love
Have nourish'd. And, for each, eternal health
Descendeth here.
Look! look! as yon deep veil
Is swept aside. what an o'erwhelming page
Disease hath written with its pen of pain.
Ah, suffering sister, thou art hasting where
No treacherous hectic plants its funeral rose:
Drink thou the wine-cup of thy risen Lord,
And it shall nerve thee for thy toilsome path
Through the dark valley of the shade of death.

—'Tis o'er. A holy silence reigns around.
The organ slumbers. The sweet, solemn voice
Of him who dealt the soul its heavenly food
Turns inward, like a wearied sentinel.
Pillowing on thought profound.
Then every head
Bends low in parting worship,—mute, and deep
The whisper of the soul. And who may tell

In that brief, silent space, how many a hope
Is born that hath a life beyond the tomb.

—So hear us, Father! in our voiceless prayer,
That at thy better banquet all may meet,
And take the cup of bliss, and thirst no more.

THOUGHTS AT THE FUNERAL OF A FRIEND.

That solemn knell, whose mournful call
Strikes on the heart, I heard;
I saw the sable pall
Covering the form revered.
And, lo! his fathers' race, the ancient and the blest,
Unlock the dim sepulchral halls, where silently they rest,
And to the unsaluting tomb,
Curtained round with rayless gloom,
He entereth in, a wearied guest.

To his bereaved abode, the fire-side chair
The holy, household prayer,
Affection's watchful zeal, his life that blest,
The tuneful lips that soothed his pain,
With the dear name of "Father" thrilling through his breast,
He cometh not again.

Flowers in his home bloom fair,
The evening taper sparkles clear,
The intellectual banquet waiteth there,
Which his heart held so dear.
The tenderness and grace
That make religion beautiful still spread
Their sainted wings to guard the place—
Alluring friendship's frequent tread.
Still seeks the stranger's foot that hospitable door,
But he, the husband and the sire, returneth never more.

His was the upright deed,
His the unswerving course,
'Mid every thwarting current's force,
Unchanged by venal aim, or flattery's hollow reed:
The holy truth walked ever by his side,
And in his bosom dwelt, companion, judge, and guide.

But when disease revealed
To his unclouded eye
The stern destroyer standing nigh,
Where turned he for a shield?
Wrapt he the robe of stainless rectitude
Around his breast to meet cold Jordan's flood?
Grasped he the staff of pride
His steps through death's dark vale to guide?

Ah no! self-righteousness he cast aside.
Clasping, with firm and fearless faith, the cross
of Him who died.

Serene,—serene,—
He press'd the crumbling verge of this terrestrial
scene,
Breath'd soft in childlike trust
The parting groan,—
Gave back to dust its dust —
To Heaven, its own.

ON A PICTURE OF PENITENCE.

Yes! look to Heaven. Earth scorns to lend
  Refuge, or stay thy steps to guide;
Bids pity with suspicion blend,
  And slander check compassion's tide.

We will not ask, what thorn hath found
  Admittance to thy bosom fair,—
If love hath dealt a traitor's wound,
  Or hopeless folly woke despair :—

We only say, that sinless clime,
  To which is raised thy streaming eye,
Hath pardon for the deepest crime,
  Though erring man that boon deny :—

We only say, the prayerful breast,
  The gushing tear of contrite pain,
Have power to ope that portal blest,
  Where vaunting pride must toil in vain.

ROME.

'Tis sunset on the Palatine. A flood
Of living glory wraps the Sabine hills,
And o'er the rough and serrate Appenines
Floats like a burning mantle. Purple mists
Rise faintly o'er the grey and ivied tombs
Of the Campagna, as sad memory steals
Forth from the twilight of the heart, to hold
Its mournful vigil o'er affection's dust.
Was that thy camp, old Romulus, where creeps
The clinging vine-flower round yon fallen fanes
And mouldering columns?
Lo! thy clay-built huts,
And band of malcontents, with barbarous port,
Up from the sea of buried ages rise,
Darkening the scene. Methinks I see thee stand,
Thou wolf-nursed monarch, o'er the human herd
Supreme in savageness, yet strong to plant
Barrier and bulwark, whence should burst a might
And majesty by thy untutored soul

Unmeasured, unconceived. As little dreams
The careless boy, who to the teeming earth
Casts the light acorn, of the forest's pomp,
Which, springing from that noteless germ, shall rear
Its banner to the skies, when he must sleep
A noteless atom.
Hark! the owlet's cry,
That, like a muttering sybil, makes her cell
Mid Nero's house of gold, with clustering bats,
And gliding lizards. Tells she not to man,
In the hoarse plaint of that discordant shriek,
The end of earthly glory?
With mad haste
No more the chariot round the stadium flies;
Nor toil the rivals in the painful race
To the far goal; nor from yon broken arch
Comes forth the victor, with flushed brow, to claim
The hard-earned garland. All have pass'd away,
Save the dead ruins, and the living robe
That nature wraps around them. Anxious fear,
High-swollen expectancy, intense despair,
And wild exulting triumph, here have reigned
And perished all.

'Twere well could we forget
How oft the gladiator's blood hath stained
Yon grass-grown pavement, while imperial
Rome
With all her fairest, brightest brows, looked
down
On the stern courage of the wounded wretch
Grappling with mortal agony. The sigh
Or tone of tender pity were to him
A dialect unknown, o'er whose dim eye
The distant vision of his cabin rude,
With all its echoing voices, all the rush
Of its cool, flowing waters, brought a pang
To which keen death was slight.
But now the scene
Once proudly peopled with the gods of earth
Spreads unempurpled, unimpassion'd forth,
While, curtain'd with her ancient glory,—Rome
Slumbereth, like one o'erwearied.

DEPARTURE OF

MRS. HANNAH MORE

FROM BARLEY WOOD.

It was a lovely scene,
That cottage 'mid the trees,
And peerless England's shaven green,
Peep'd, their interstices between,
While in each sweet recess, and grotto wild,
Nature convers'd with art, or on her labours smil'd.

It seem'd a parting hour,
And she whose hand had made
That spot so beautiful with woven shade
And aromatic shrub and flower,
Turn'd her from those haunts away,
Tho' spring relum'd each charm, and fondly woo'd her stay.

Yon mansion teems with legends for the
heart:
There her lov'd sisters circled round her side,
To share in all her toils a part,
There, too, with gentle sigh
Each laid her down to die:
Methinks their beckoning phantoms glide,
Twining with tenderest ties
Of hoarded memories,
Green bower, and quiet walk, and vine wreath'd
spot:
Hark! where the cypress waves
Above their peaceful graves,
Seems not some echo on the gale to rise?
"O, sister, leave us not!"

Her lingering footstep stays
Upon that threshold stone,
And o'er the pictur'd wall, her farewell gaze
Rests on the portraits, one by one,
Of treasur'd friends, before her gone
To that bright world of bliss where partings are
unknown.

The wintry snows
That fourscore years disclose,
When slow to life's last verge, Time's lonely
chariot goes,
Are on her temples; and her features meek

Subdued and silent sorrow speak;
Yet still her arm in cheerful trust doth lean
On faithful friendship's prop,—that changeless
evergreen.

Like Eve, from Paradise, she goes,
Yet not by guilt involv'd in woes,
Nor driven by angel bands,—
The flaming sword is planted at her gate
By menial hands:
Yes, those who at her table fed
Despise the giver of their daily bread
And from ingratitude and hate
The wounded patron fled.

Think not the pang was slight
That thus within her uncomplaining breast
She cover'd from the light:
Tho' knowledge o'er her mind had pour'd
The full, imperishable hoard,
Tho' virtue, such as dwells among the blest,
Came nightly, on reflection's wing, to soothe her
soul to rest,
Tho' Fame to farthest earth her name had
borne,
These brought no shield against the envious
thorn:
Deem not the envenom'd dart
Invulnerable found her thrilling woman's heart.

Man's home is everywhere. On ocean's flood,
Where the strong ship with storm-defying tether
Doth link in stormy brotherhood
Earth's utmost zones together,
Where'er the red gold glows, the spice-trees wave,
Where the rich diamond ripens, 'mid the flame
Of vertic suns that ope the stranger's grave,
He, with bronz'd cheek and daring step doth rove;
He with short pang and slight
Doth turn him from the chequer'd light
Of the fair moon thro' his own forests dancing,
Where music, joy, and love,
Were his young hours entrancing;
And where ambition's thunder-claim
Points out his lot,
Or fitful wealth allures to roam,
There, doth he make his home,
Repining not.

It is not thus with Woman. The far halls,
Though ruinous and lone,
Where first her pleased ear drank a nursing mother's tone,—
The home with humble walls,
Where breath'd a parent's prayer around her bed,—
The valley, where with playmates true,
She cull'd the strawberry, bright with dew,—

The bower, where Love her timid footsteps
led,—
The hearth-stone where her children grew,—
The damp soil where she cast
The flower-seeds of her hope, and saw them
bide the blast,—
Affection, with unfading tint recalls,
Lingering round the ivied walls,
Where every rose hath in its cup a bee,
Making fresh honey of remember'd things,
Each rose without a thorn, each bee bereft of
stings.

PEACE.

"Peace I leave with you."—JOHN, xiv., 27.

"*Peace*," was the song the angels sang,
  When Jesus sought this vale of tears,
And sweet that heavenly prelude rang,
  To calm the wondering shepherds' fears:—
"*War*," is the word that man hath spoke,
  Convuls'd by passions dark and dread,
And vengeance bound a lawless yoke
  Even where the Gospel's banner spread

"*Peace*," was the prayer the Saviour breathed
  When from our world his steps withdrew,
The gift he to his friends bequeathed
  With Calvary and the cross in view:—
And ye whose souls have felt his love,
  Guard day and night this rich bequest,
The watch-word of the host above,
  The passport to their realm of rest.

TOMB OF A YOUNG FRIEND AT MOUNT AUBURN.

I DO remember thee.
There was a strain
Of thrilling music, a soft breath of flowers
Telling of summer to a festive throng,
That fill'd the lighted halls. And the sweet smile
That spoke their welcome, the high warbled lay
Swelling with rapture through a parent's heart,
Were thine.
Time wav'd his noiseless wand awhile,
And in thy cherish'd home once more I stood,
Amid those twin'd and cluster'd sympathies
Where the rich blessings of thy heart sprang forth,
Like the moss rose. Where was the voice of song
Pouring out glad and glorious melody?—
But when I ask'd for thee, they took me where
A hallow'd mountain wrapt its verdant head
In changeful drapery of woods, and flowers,

And silver streams, and where thou erst didst love,
Musing to walk, and lend a serious ear
To the wild melody of birds that hung
Their unharm'd dwellings 'mid its woven bowers.
Yet here and there, involv'd in curtaining shades
Uprose those sculptur'd monuments that bear
The ponderous warnings of eternity.

So, thou hast pass'd the unreturning gate,
Where dust with dust doth linger, and gone down
In all the beauty of thy blooming years
To this most sacred city of the dead.
The granite obelisk and the pale flower
Reveal thy couch. Fit emblems of the frail
And the immortal.
But that bitter grief
Which holds stern vigil o'er the mouldering clay,
Keeping long night-watch with its sullen lamp
Had fled thy tomb, and faith did lift its eye
Full of sweet tears: for when warm tear-drops gush
From the pure memories of a love that wrought
For others happiness, and rose to take
Its own full share of happiness above,
Are they not sweet?

MIDNIGHT MUSIC.*

WHAT maketh music, when the bird
  Doth hush its merry lay?
And the sweet spirit of the flowers
  Hath sighed itself away?
What maketh music when the frost
  Enchains the murmuring rill,
And every song that summer woke
  In winter's trance is still?

* "The Rev. Mr. George Herbert, in one of his walks to Salisbury to join a musical society, saw a poor man, with a poorer horse, which had fallen under its load. Putting off his canonical coat, he helped the poor man to unload, and raise the horse, and afterwards to load him again. The poor man blessed him for it, and he blessed the poor man. And so like was he to the good Samaritan, that he gave him money to refresh both himself and his horse, admonishing him also, 'if he loved himself, to be merciful to his beast.' Then, coming to his musical friends at Salisbury, they began to wonder that Mr. George Herbert, who used to be always so trim and neat, should come into that company so soiled and

What maketh music when the winds
In strong encounter rise,
When ocean strikes his thunder-gong,
And the rent cloud replies?
While no adventurous planet dares
The midnight arch to deck,
And, in its startled dream, the babe
Doth clasp its mother's neck?

And when the fiercer storms of fate
Wild o'er the pilgrim sweep,
And earthquake-voices claim the hopes
He treasur'd long and deep,
When loud the threatening passions roar
Like lions in their den,
And vengeful tempests lash the shore,
What maketh music then?

---

discomposed. Yet, when he told them the reason, one of them said that he had 'disparaged himself by so mean an employment.' But his answer was that the thought of what he had done, would prove *music to him at midnight*, and that the omission of it would have made discord in his conscience, whenever he should pass that place. 'For if,' said he, 'I am bound to *pray* for all that are in distress, I am surely bound, so far as is in my power, to *practise* what I pray for. And though I do not wish for the like occasion every day, yet would I not willingly pass one day of my life without comforting a sad soul, or showing mercy, and I praise God for this opportunity. So now let us tune our instruments' "

The deed to humble virtue born.
  Which nursing memory taught
To shun a boastful world's applause,
  And love the lowly thought,
This builds a cell within the heart,
  Amid the blasts of care
And tuning high its heaven-struck harp,
  Makes midnight music there.

TRUST IN GOD.

"And David said, Let me now fall into the hand of the Lord, for his mercies are great,—and let me not fall into the hand of man."—2 Sam. xxiv., 14.

Man hath a voice severe,
His neighbour's fault to blame,
A wakeful eye, a listening ear
To note his brother's shame.

He, with suspicious glance
The curtain'd breast doth read,
And raise the accusing balance high,
To weigh the doubtful deed.

Oh Thou, whose piercing thought
Doth note each secret path,
For mercy to Thy throne, we fly,
From man's condemning wrath.

Thou, who dost dimness mark
In Heaven's resplendent way,

And folly in that angel host
  Who serve thee night and day.

How fearless should our trust
  In thy compassion be,
When from our brother of the dust
  We dare appeal to Thee.

THE CHRISTIAN MOURNER.

I SAW a dark procession slowly wind
'Mid funeral shades, and a lone mourner stand
Fast by the yawning of the pit that whelm'd
His bosom's idol.
Then the sable scene
Faded away, and to his alter'd home
Sad fancy follow'd him, and saw him fold
His one, lone babe, in agoniz'd embrace,
And kiss the brow of trusting innocence,
That in its blessed ignorance wail'd not
A mother lost. Yet she who would have watch'd
Each germ of intellect, each bud of truth,
Each fair unfolding of the fruit of Heaven,
With thrilling joy, was like the marble cold.

—There were the flowers she planted, blooming fair,
As if in mockery,—there the varied stores
That in the beauty of their order charm'd
At once the tasteful and the studious hour,
Pictures, and tinted shells, and treasur'd tomes;

But the presiding mind, the cheerful voice,
The greeting glance, the spirit-stirring smile,
Fled, fled for ever.
And he knoweth all!
Hath felt it all, deep in his tortur'd soul,
Till reason and philosophy grew faint,
Beneath a grief like his. Whence hath he then
The power to comfort others, and to speak
Thus of the resurrection?
He hath found
That hope which is an anchor to the soul,
And with a martyr-courage holds him up
To bear the will of God.
Say, ye who tempt
The sea of life, by summer-gales impell'd,
Have ye this anchor? Sure a time will come
For storms to try you, and strong blasts to rend
Your painted sails, and shred your gold-like chaff
O'er the wild wave; and what a wreck is man
If sorrow find him unsustain'd by God.

FAITH.

WRAPT in the robe of Faith,
  Come to the place of prayer,
And seal thy deathless vows to Him
  Who makes thy life his care.

Doth he thy sunny skies
  O'ercloud with tempest gloom?
Or take the idol of thy breast,
  And hide it in the tomb?

Or bid thy treasur'd joys
  In hopeless ruin lie?
Search not his reasons,—wait his will;
  The record is on high.

For should he strip thy heart
  Of all it boasts on earth,
And set thee naked and alone,
  As at thy day of birth,

He cannot do thee wrong,
  Those gifts were his at first,—

FAITH.

Draw nearer to his changeless throne,
  Bow deeper in the dust.

Calls he thy parting soul
  Unbodied from the throng?
Cling closer to thy Saviour's cross
  And raise the victor song.

THE DYING MOTHER'S PRAYER.

I HEARD the voice of prayer—a mother's prayer—
A dying mother for her only son.
Young was his brow, and fair.
Her hand was on his head,
Her words of love were said,
Her work was done.

And there were other voices near her bed—
Sweet, bird-like voices—for their mother dear
Asking, with mournful tear.
Ah, by whose hand shall those sad tears be dried,
When one brief hour is fled,
And hers shall pulseless rest, low with the silent dead?

Yes, there was death's dark valley, drear and cold!
And the hoarse dash of an o'erwhelming wave
Alone she treads: is there no earthly hold,
No friend—no helper- no strong arm to save?

Down to the fearful grave,
In the firm courage of a faith serene,
Alone she press'd—
And as she drew the chord
That bound her to her Lord
More closely round her breast,
The white wing of the waiting angel spread
More palpably, and earth's bright things grew
pale.
Even fond affection's wail
Seemed like the far-off sigh of spring's forgotten
gale.

And so the mother's prayer,
So often breathed above,
In agonizing love,
Rose high in praise of God's protecting care.
Meek on his arm her infant charge she laid,
And with a trusting eye,
Of Christian constancy,
Confiding in her blest Redeemer's aid,
She taught the weeping band,
Who round her couch of pain did stand,
How a weak woman's hand,
Fettered with sorrow and with sin,
Might from the king of terrors win
The victory.

CONSECRATION OF A CHURCH.

Lift up your heads, ye hallowed gates, and give
The King of Glory room."
And then a strain
Of solemn trembling melody inquired,
" Who is the King of Glory."
But a sound
Brake from the echoing temple, like the rush
Of many waters, blent with organ's breath,
And the soul's harp, and the uplifted voice
Of prelate, and of people, and of priest,
Responding joyously—" The Lord of Hosts,
He is the King of Glory."
Enter in
To this his new abode, and with glad heart
Kneel low before his footstool. Supplicate
That favouring presence which doth condescend,
From the pavilion of high heaven to beam
On earthly temples, and in contrite souls.

Here fade all vain distinctions that the pride
Of man can arrogate. This house of prayer

Doth teach that all are sinners—all have strayed
Like erring sheep. The princely, or the poor,
The bright or ebon brow, the pomp of power,
The boast of intellect, what are they here?
Man sinks to nothing, while he deals with God.

Yet, let the grateful hymn of those who share
A boundless tide of blessings—those who tread
Their pilgrim path, rejoicing in the hope
Of an ascended Saviour—through these walls
For ever flow. Thou dedicated dome!
May'st thou in majesty and beauty stand:
Stand, and give praise, until the rock-ribbed
earth
In her last throes shall tremble. Then dissolve
Into thy native dust, with one long sigh
Of melody, while the redeemed souls
That, 'neath thine arch, to endless life were
born,
Go up, on wings of glory, to the "house
Not made with hands."

THE CHRISTIAN GOING HOME.

Occasioned by the words of a dying friend,—"Before morning, I shall be at home."

HOME! home! its glorious threshold
Through parted clouds I see,
Those mansions by a Saviour bought,
Where I have longed to be,
And, lo! a bright unnumbered host
O'erspread the heavenly plain,
Not one is silent—every harp
Doth swell the adoring strain.

Fain would my soul be praising
Amid that sinless throng,
Fain would my voice be raising
Their everlasting song,—
Hark! hark! they bid me hasten
To leave the fainting clay,
Friends! hear ye not the welcome sound!
"Arise, and co ne away."

Before the dawn of morning
  These lower skies shall light,
I shall have joined their company
  Above this realm of night,
Give thanks, my mourning dear ones,
  Thanks to the Eternal King,
Who crowns my soul with victory
  And plucks from Death the sting.

WAITING UPON THE LORD.

"I will wait upon the Lord, that hideth his face."
ISAIAH.

WHERE'ER thine earthly lot is cast,
  Whate'er its duties prove,
To toil 'neath penury's piercing blast,
  Or share the cell of love,
Or 'mid the pomp of wealth to live,
  Or wield of power the rod,
Still as a faithful servant strive
  To wait alone on God.

Should disappointment's blighting sway
  Destroy of joy the bloom,
Till one by one thy hopes decay
  In darkness and the tomb,
Should Heaven its cheering smile withhold
  From thy disastrous fate,
And foes arise like billows bold,—
  Still, on Jehovah wait.

When timid dawn her couch forsakes,
  Or noon-day splendours glide,
Or eve her curtain'd pillow takes,
  While watchful stars preside,
Or midnight drives the throngs of care
  Far from her ebon throne,
Unwearied in thy fervent prayer
  Wait thou on God alone.

But should He still conceal his face
  Till flesh and spirit fail,
And bid thee darkly run the race
  Of Time's receding vale,
With what a doubly glorious ray
  His smile will light that sky
Where ransom'd souls rejoicing lay
  Their robes of mourning by

DEATH-BED OF THE REV. DR. PAYSON.

"The eye spoke after the tongue became motionless. Looking on his wife, and glancing over the others who surrounded his bed, it rested on his eldest son, with an expression which was interpreted by all present to say, as plainly as if he had uttered the words of the beloved disciple,—'Behold thy mother!'"

Memoir of the Rev. Edward Payson.

WHAT said the eye? The marble lip spake not,
Save in that quivering sob with which stern death
Crusheth life's harp-strings. Lo! again it pours
A tide of more than uttered eloquence—
"Son! look upon thy mother,"—and retires
Beneath the curtain of the drooping lids
To hide itself for ever. 'Tis the last,
Last glance! and, ah! how tenderly it fell
Upon that loved companion, and the groups

Who wept around. Full well the dying knew
The value of those holy charities
Which purge the dross of selfishness away;
And deep he felt that woman's trusting heart
Rent from the cherished prop which, next to
Christ,
Had been her stay in all adversities,
Would take the balm-cup best from that dear
hand
Which woke the sources of maternal love;
That smile whose winning paid for sleepless
nights
Of cradle-care—that voice whose murmured
tones
Her own had moulded to the words of prayer.
How soothing to a widowed mother's breast,
Her first-born's sympathy.
Be strong, young man
Lift the protector's arm, the healer's prayer—
Be tender in thine every word and deed.
A spirit watcheth thee! Yes, he who pass'd
From shaded earth up to the full-orbed day,
Will be thy witness in the court of Heaven,
How thou dost bear his mantle. So, farewell,
Leader in Israel! Thou whose radiant path
Was like the angel's standing* in the sun,
Undazzled and unswerving. It was meet
That thou should'st rise to light without a cloud.

* Revelations, xix., 17.

MISSION HYMN.

Onward! onward! men of heaven,
Rear the Gospel's banner high;
Rest not, till its light is given,—
Star of every pagan sky.
Bear it where the pilgrim-stranger
Faints 'neath Asia's vertic ray;
Bid the red-browed forest-ranger
Hail it, ere he fades away.

Where the arctic ocean thunders,—
Where the tropics fiercely glow,
Broadly spread its page of wonders
Brightly bids its radiance flow.
India marks its lustre, stealing,
Shivering Greenland loves its rays,
Afric, 'mid her deserts kneeling,
Lifts the untaught strain of praise.

Rude in speech, or grim in feature,
Dark in spirit though they be,
Show that light to every creature,—
Prince or vassal,—bond or free.—

Lo! they haste to every nation;
  Host on host the ranks supply;
Onward! Christ is your salvation,
  And your death is victory!

ON MEETING SEVERAL FORMER PUPILS AT THE COMMUNION TABLE.

"I have no greater joy than to see my children walk in the truth."—St. John.

When kneeling round a Saviour's board
  Fair forms, and brows belov'd, I see,
Who once the paths of peace explor'd,
  And trac'd the studious page with me,—

Who from my side with pain would part;
  My entering step with gladness greet,
And pour complacent, o'er my heart,
  Affection's dew-drops, pure and sweet,

When now, from each remember'd face
  Beam tranquil hope and trust benign,
When in each eye Heaven's smile I trace,
  The tear of joy suffuses mine.

Father! I bless thy ceaseless care,
  Which thus its holiest gifts hath shed;
Guide Thou their steps through every snare,
  From every danger shield their head.

From treacherous error's dire control,—
  From pride, from change, from darkness free
Preserve each timorous, trusting soul,
  That, like the ark-dove, flies to Thee.

And may the wreath that cloudless days
  Around our hearts so fondly wove,
Still bind us till we speak Thy praise,
  As sister spirits, one in love;—

One, where no lingering ill can harm;
  One, where no stroke of fate can sever;
Where nought but holiness doth charm,
  And all that charms shall live for ever.

THE LOST SISTER.

THEY wak'd me from my sleep, I knew not
 why,
And bade me hasten where a midnight lamp
Gleam'd from an inner chamber. There she
 lay,
With brow so pale,—who yester-morn breath'd
 forth
Through joyous smiles her superflux of bliss
Into the hearts of others. By her side
Her hoary sire, with speechless sorrow, gazed
Upon the stricken idol,—all dismay'd
Beneath his God's rebuke. And she who nurs'd
That fair young creature at her gentle breast,
And oft those sunny locks had deck'd with buds
Of rose and jasmine, shuddering wip'd the dews
Which death distils.
 The sufferer just had given
Her long farewell, and for the last, *last* time
Touch'd with cold lips his cheek who led so late
Her footsteps to the altar, and receiv'd
In the deep transport of an ardent heart
Her vow of love And she had striven to press

That golden circlet with her bloodless hand
Back on his finger, which he kneeling gave
At the bright, bridal morn. So, there she lay
In calm endurance, like the smitten lamb
Wounded in flowery pastures, from whose breast
The dreaded bitterness of death had pass'd.
—But a faint wail disturb'd the silent scene,
And, in its nurse's arms a new-born babe
Was borne in utter helplessness along,
Before that dying eye.
Its gather'd film
Kindled one moment with a sudden glow
Of tearless agony,—and fearful pangs,
Racking the rigid features, told how strong
A mother's love doth root itself. One cry
Of bitter anguish, blent with fervent prayer,
Went up to Heaven,—and, as its cadence sank,
Her spirit enter'd there.
Morn after morn
Rose and retir'd; yet still as in a dream
I seem'd to move. The certainty of loss
Fell not *at once* upon me. Then I wept
As weep the sisterless.—For thou wert fled,
My only, my belov'd, my sainted one,—
Twin of my spirit! and my number'd days
Must wear the sable of that midnight hour
Which rent thee from me.

MISTAKEN GRIEF.

"There the wicked cease from troubling, and there the weary are at rest." JOB

We mourn for those who toil,
The wretch who ploughs the main,
The slave who hopeless tills the soil
Beneath the stripe and chain;
For those who in the world's hard race,
O'erwearied and unblest,
A host of gliding phantoms chase;
Why mourn for those who rest?

We mourn for those who sin,
Bound in the tempter's snare,
Whom syren pleasure beckoneth in
To prisons of despair,—
Whose hearts, by whirlwind passions torn,
Are wreck'd on folly's shore,
But why in anguish should we mourn
For those who sin no more?

We mourn for those who weep
  Whom stern afflictions bend,
Despairing o'er the lowly sleep
  Of lover or of friend;
But they who Jordan's swelling tide
  No more are call'd to stem,
Whose tears the hand of God hath dried
  Why should we mourn for them?

DEPARTURE OF MISSIONARIES FOR CEYLON.

Wave, wide Ceylon, your foliage fair,
  Your spicy fragrance freely strew,
See, ocean's threatening surge we dare,
  To bear salvation's gift to you.

And, ye who long with faithful hand
  Have fondly till'd that favour'd soil,
We come, we come, a brother-band
  To share the burden of your toil.

Land of our birth! we may not stay
  The ardour of our hearts to tell,
Friends of our youth! we dare not say
  How deep within our souls ye dwell.

But when the dead, both small and great,
  Shall stand before the Judge's seat,
When sea, and sky, and earthly state,
  All like a baseless vision fleet,

The hope that then some heathen eye
  Thro' us, an angel's glance may raise,
Bids us to vanquish nature's tie,
  And turn her parting tear to praise.

CRY OF THE CORANNAS.

"Missionaries are going far beyond us,—but they come not to us. We have been promised a missionary, but can get none. God has given us plenty of corn, but we are perishing for want of instruction. Our people are dying every day. We have heard there is another life after death, but we know nothing of it."

We see our infants fade. The mother clasps
The enfeebled form, and watches night and day
Its speechless agony, with tears and cries,
But there's a hand more strong than her despair,
That rends it from her bosom. Our young men
Are bold and full of strength, but something comes,
We know not what, and so they droop and die.
Those whom we lov'd so much, our gentler friends,
Who bless our homes, *we gaze, and they are gone.*

Our mighty chiefs, who in the battle's rage
Tower'd up like gods, so fearless, and return'd
So loftily, behold! they pine away
Like a pale girl, and so, we lay them down
With the forgotten throng, who dwell in dust.

They call it death, and we have faintly heard
By a far echo o'er the distant sea
There was a life beyond it. *Is it so?*
If there be aught above this mouldering mound
Where we do leave our friends,—if there be hope,
So passing strange, that they should rise again
And we should see them, we who mourn them now,
We pray you speak such glorious tidings forth
In our benighted clime. Ye heaven-spread sails
Pass us not by! Men of the living God!
Upon our mountain-heights we stand and shout
To you in our distress. Fain would we hear
Your wondrous message fully, that our hearts
May hail its certainty, before we go
Ourselves to those dark caverns of the dead,
Where everlasting silence seems to reign.

GIFT OF A BIBLE.

Behold the book,—o'er which, from ancient time,
  Sad penitence hath poured the prayerful breath,
And meek devotion bowed with joy sublime,
  And nature armed her for the strife of death,
And trembling hope renewed her wreath divine,
And faith an anchor gained:—that holy book is thine.

Behold the book,—whose sacred truths to spread
  Christ's heralds toil beneath a foreign sky,
Pouring its blessings o'er the heathen's head,
  A martyr-courage kindling in their eye.
Wide o'er the globe its glorious light must shine,
As glows the arch of heaven:—that holy book is thine.

Here search with humble heart, and ardent eye,
  Where plants of peace in bloom celestial grow;

Here breathe to mercy's ear the contrite sigh,
  And bid the soul's unsullied fragrance flow
To Him who shuts the rose at even-tide,
And opes its dewy eye when earliest sunbeams
    glide

May Heaven's pure Spirit touch thy soften'd
    heart,
  And guide thy feet through life's eventful lot:
That when from this illusive scene I part,
  And in the grave lie mouldering and forgot,
This, my first gift, like golden link, may join
Thee, to that angel-band around the Throne
    Divine.

HOME MISSIONS.

Turn thee to thine own broad waters,
Labor in thy native earth,
Call salvation's sons and daughters
From the clime that gave thee birth.

Here are pilgrim-souls benighted,
Here are evils to be slain,
Graces in their budding blighted,
Spirits bound in error's chain.

Raise the Gospel's glorious streamer
Where yon cloud-topp'd forest waves,
Follower of the meek Redeemer
Serve him 'mid thy father's graves.

ON THE DEATH OF A FRIEND.

SHE passeth hence,—a friend from loving friends,
A mother from her children. Time hath shed
No frost upon her, and the tree of life
Glows in the freshness of its summer prime.—
Yet still she passeth hence : her work on earth
Soon done, and well. Her's was the unwavering mind,
The untiring hand in duty. Firm of soul
And pure in purpose, on the Eternal Rock
Of Christian trust, her energies reposed,
And sought no tribute from a shadowy world.
Her early hope and homage clave to God,
When the bright skies, the untroubled founts of youth,
With all their song-birds, all their flowers, rose up
To tempt her spirit. So, in hours of pain,
He did remember her, and on her brow
And in her breast, the dove-like messenger
Found peaceful home.
O thou, whom grieving love
Would blindly pinion in this vale of tears,

Farewell! It is a glorious flight for faith
To trace thy upward path, above this clime
Of change and storm. We will remember thee
At thy turf-bed,—and, 'mid the twilight hour
Of solemn music, when the buried friend
Comes back so visibly, and seems to fill
The vacant chair, our speech shall be of thee.

THE JOURNEY WITH THE DEAD.

They journey 'neath the summer sky,
  A lov'd and loving train,
But Nature spreads her genial charms
  To lure their souls in vain,
Husband and wife and child are there,
  Warm-hearted, true and kind,
Yet every kindred lip is seal'd,
  And every head declin'd.

Weary and sad, their course is bent
  To seek an ancient dome,
Where hospitality hath made
  A long-remember'd home;
And one with mournful care they bring
  Whose footstep erst was gay
Amid these halls; why comes she now
  In sorrow's dark array?

Here fell a sainted grandsire's prayer
  Upon her infant rest,
And with the love of ripen'd years
  The cherish'd haunt was blest,

Here was the talisman that bade
  Her heart's blood sparkle high,
Why steals no flush across her cheek?
  No lightning to her eye?

They bear her to the house of God,
  But though that hallow'd spot
Is fill'd with prayer from lips she lov'd
  Her voice respondeth not,
She heedeth not, she heedeth not,
  She, who from early days
Had joy'd within that holy Church,
  To swell Jehovah's praise.

Then onward toward a narrow cell
  They tread the grass-grown track,
From whence the unreturning guest
  Doth send no tidings back;
There sleeps the grandsire high and brave
  In freedom's battles tried,*
With him whose banner was the cross
  Of Jesus crucified.

Down by those hoary chiefs she laid
  Her young, unfrosted head,
To rise no more, until the voice
  Of Jesus wakes the dead,

* General Putnam.

From her own dear, domestic power,
  From deep, confiding love,
From earth's unshaded smile, she turn'd
  To purer bliss above,

PRISONERS' EVENING HYMN.

WRITTEN FOR THE FEMALES IN THE CONNECTICUT STATE PRISON.

THE silent curtains of the night
  Our lonely cell surround,
God's dwelling is in perfect light,
  His mercy hath no bound.

Still on the sinful and the vile
  His daily bounties fall,
And still his sun with cheering smile
  Dispenses good to all.

The way of wickedness is hard,
  Its bitter fruits we know,
Shame in this world is its reward.
  And in the future, woe.

But Thou! who see'st us while we pay
  The penance of our guilt,
Cast not our souls condemn'd away,
  Christ's blood for us was spilt.

Deep root within a soil subdued
  Let true repentance take,
And be its fruits a life renew'd,
  For the Redeemer's sake.

Uplift our spirits from the ground,
  Give to our darkness, light.
Oh thou! whose mercies have no bound,
  Preserve us safe this night.

THE HUGUENOT PASTOR.

During the persecution of the Huguenots in France, soon after the revocation of the edict of Nantz, one of their ministers, possessed of great learning and piety, having witnessed the demolition of his own Church at Montpelier, was induced by the solicitations of his people, to preach to them in the night, upon its ruins. For this offence, he was condemned to be broken on the wheel.

Behold him on the ruins, not of fanes
With ivy mantled, which the touch of time
Hath slowly crumbled,—but amid the wreck
Of his own temple, by infuriate hands
In shapeless masses, and rude fragments strown
Wide o'er the trampled turf. Serene he stood,
A pale, sad beauty on his youthful brow,
With eyes uprais'd, as if his stricken soul
Fled from material things. Where was the spire
That solemn through those chestnut trees looked forth?
The tower, the arch, the altar, whence he bless'd

A kneeling throng? the font where infancy
Rais'd in his arms to God was consecrate,
An incense-breathing bud? Not on such themes
Dar'd his fond thoughts to dwell, but firm in faith
He lifted up his voice and spake of Heaven,
Where desolations come not.
Midnight hung
Dreary and dense around, and the lone lamp
That o'er his Bible stream'd, hung tremulous
Beneath the fitful gale.
There, resting deep
Upon the planted staff, were aged men,
The grave's white tokens in their scatter'd hair.
And youthful forms, with gaze intensely fix'd
On their beloved Pastor, as he taught
Of Christ their righteousness, while here and there
A group of mourning mothers from whose arms
Their babes by persecution's rage were torn
Blent with their listening, the low sob of grief.
Close by their father's knees young children cower'd
And in each echoing footstep fear'd a foe.
—It was a time of trouble, and the flock
Came hungering for the heavenly bread which gives
Strength to the heavy laden. 'Twas a scene
That France might well have wept with tears of blood

But in the madness of a dire disease
She slew her loyal sons, and urg'd the sword
'Gainst her own vitals.
Lo! the dawn is out,
With her grey banner, and the parting flock
Seek their own homes, praising the Hand tha spares
Their faithful shepherd. Silent evening wakes
Far different orgies. Yonder mangled form
Sinking 'neath murderous fury, can ye trace
Its lineaments of beauty, 'mid the wreck
Of anguish and distortion? Son of God!
Is this *thy* messenger, whose voice so late
Thrill'd with an angel's sweetness, as it pour'd
Thy blessing on the people?
Yet, be still,
And breathe no bitter thought above his dust,
Who served the Prince of Peace. The spirit of love
Did make that lifeless breast its temple-shrine,
Offend it not. But raise with tender hand
Those blood-stain'd curls, and shed the pitying tear.
—That marble lip no more can bless its foes,
But from the wreck of martyrdom, the soul
Hath risen n radiance, o'er the strife of man.

"THIS IS NOT YOUR REST."

WHEN Heaven s unerring pencil writes, on every
pilgrim's breast,
Its passport to Time's changeful shore, "*lo, this
is not your rest,*"
Why build ye towers, ye fleeting ones? why
bowers of fragrance rear?
As if the self-deceiving soul might find its Eden
here.

In vain! In vain! wild storms will rise and o'er
your fabrics sweep,
Yet when loud thunders wake the wave, and
deep replies to deep,
When in your path, Hope's broken prism doth
shed its parting ray,
Spring up and fix your tearful eye on undeclining
day.

If like an ice-bolt to the heart, frail Friendship's
altered eye
Admits those rosy wreaths are dead, it promis'd
could not die,

Lift, lift to an Eternal Friend, the agonizing prayer,
The souls that put their trust in Him, shall never know despair.

If Fancy, she who bids young Thought, its freshest incense bring,
By stern reality rebuk'd, should fold her stricken wing,
There is a brighter, broader realm than she has yet reveal'd,
From flesh-girt man's exploring eye, and anxious ear conceal'd.

Earth is Death's palace: to his court he summons great and small,
The crown'd, the homeless and the slave, are but his minions all;
We turn us shrinking from the truth, the close pursuit we fly,
But faulter on the grave's dark brink, and lay us down and die.

THE SECOND BIRTH-DAY.

Thou dost not dream, my little one,
  How great the change must be,
These two years, since the morning sun
  First shed his beams on thee;
Thy little hands did helpless fall,
  As with a stranger's fear,
And a faint wailing cry was all
  That met thy mother's ear.

But now the dictates of thy will
  Thine active feet obey,
And, pleased, thy busy fingers still
  Among thy playthings stray;
And thy full eyes delighted rove
  The pictured page along,
And, lisping to the heart of love,
  Thy thousand wishes throng.

Fair boy! the wanderings of thy way,
  It is not mine to trace:
Through buoyant youth's exulting day
  Or manhood's bolder race:

What discipline thy heart may need,
What clouds may veil thy sun,
The eye of God alone can read—
And let his will be done.

Yet might a mother's prayer of love
Thy destiny control,
Those boasted gifts that often prove
The ruin of the soul,
Beauty and fortune, wit and fame,
For thee it would not crave,
But tearful urge a fervent claim
To joys beyond the grave.

O! be thy wealth an upright heart,
Thy strength the sufferer's stay,
Thine early choice, that better part,
Which cannot fade away;
Thy zeal for Christ a quenchless fire,
Thy friends the men of peace,
Thy heritage an angel's lyre,
When earthly changes cease

DEATH OF A CLERGYMAN.

So, from the field of labour thou art gone
To thy reward,—like him who putteth off
His outer garment, at the noontide hour,
To take a quiet sleep. Thy zeal hath run
Its course untiring, and thy quicken'd love,
Where'er thy Master pointed, joy'd to go.

—Amid thy faithful toil, His summons came,
Warning thee home,—and thou didst loose thy heart
From thy fond flock, and from affection's bonds
And from thy blessed children's warm embrace,
With smiles and songs of praise.
Death smote thee sore,
And plung'd his keen shaft in the quivering nerve,
Making the breath that stirr'd life's broken valve
A torturing gasp, but with thy martyrdom
Were smiles and songs of praise.

And thou didst rise
Above the pealing of these sabbath bells
Up to that glorious and unspotted church
Whose worship is eternal.
Would that all
Who love our Lord might with thy welcome look
On the last foe,—not as a spoiler, sent
To wreck their treasures and to blast their joys,
But as a friend, who wraps the weary clay
With earth, its mother, and doth raise the soul
To that blest consummation, which its prayers
Unceasingly besought,—tho' its best hopes
But faintly shadow'd forth.
So, tho' we hear
Thy voice on earth no more,—the holy hymn
With which thou down to Jordan's shore didst go
To take thy last, cold baptism, still shall waft
As from some cloud, its echoed sweetness back
To teach us of the melody of heaven.

"DEPART, CHRISTIAN SOUL."

Depart! depart! the silver cord is breaking,
The sun-ray fades before the darken'd sight
The subtle essence from the clod is taking,
'Mid groans and pangs, its everlasting flight,
Lingerest thou fearful? Christ the grave hath bless'd,
He in that lowly couch did deign to take his rest.

Depart! thy sojourn here hath been in sorrow.
Tears were thy meat along the thorn-clad path,
The hope of eve was but a clouded morrow,
And sin appall'd thee with thy Maker's wrath,
Earth gave her lessons in a tempest-voice.
Thy discipline is ended. Chasten'd one, rejoice!

Thou wert a stranger here, and all thy trouble
To bind a wreath upon the brow of pain,

To build a bower upon the watery bubble,
Or strike an anchor 'neath its depths, was vain;
Depart! depart! all tears are wiped away,
The seraph-marshall'd road is toward the realm of day.

THE FOREST TRIBES.

Where are they, the forest-rangers,
  Children of this western-land?
Who, to greet the pale-fac'd strangers,
  Stretch'd the unsuspecting hand?
Where are they, whom passion goaded
  Madly to the unequal fight,
Tossing wild the feathery arrow
  'Gainst the girded warrior's might?

Were not these their own bright waters?
  Were not these their native skies?
Rear'd they not their red-brow'd daughters
  Where our princely mansions rise?
From the vale their roofs have vanish'd,
  From these streams their slight canoe;
Chieftains and their tribes have perish'd,
  Like the thickets where they grew.

Though their blood, no longer gushing,
  Wakeneth war's discordant cry,

Stains it not the maple's flushing
 When sad Autumn's step is nigh?
None are living to deplore them,—
 None survive their names to tell,—
But the sad breeze murmuring o'er them,
 Seems to sigh "farewell—farewell."

DEATH OF A DISTINGUISHED MAN.

Death's shafts are ever busy. The fair haunts
Where least we dread him, and where most the soul
Doth lull itself to fond security,
Reveal his ministry; and, were not man
Blind to the future, he might see the sky,
Even in the glory of its cloudless prime,
Dark with that arrow-flight.
They deemed it so
Who marked thee like a stately column fall,
And in the twinkling of an eye, yield back
Thy breath to Him who gave it. Yes,—they felt,
Who saw thy vigorous footstep strangely chained
Upon the turf it traversed, and the cheek,
Flushed high with health, to mortal paleness turn'd,
How awful such a rush from time must be.
Thy brow was calm, yet deep within thy breast
Were ranklings of a recent grief for her,

The idol of thy tenderness, with whom
Life had been one long scene of changeless love.
Yea, thou didst watch the winged messenger
In sleepless agony that bore her hence,—
And, when that bright eye darken'd from whose beams
Thine own had drank from youth its dearest joy,
Upraised thine hands and gave her back to God.
The bleeding of thy heart-strings was not stanched,
Nor scarce the tear-gush dried, ere death's dire frost
Congeal'd thy fount of life.

Thy toil had been,
In that brief interval, to bear fresh plants
From the sweet garden which she loved to tend,
And bid them on her burial-pillow bloom.
But, ere the young rose, or the willow-tree,
Had taken their simplest rooting, thou wert laid
Low by her side. It was a pleasant place
Methought to rest,—earth's weary labour done,
Fanned by the waving of those drooping boughs,
And in her company whom thou didst choose,
From all the world, to travel by thy side,
Confidingly,—by deep affection cheer'd,
And in thy faith a sharer.

From the haunts
Of living men, thine image may not fleet
Noteless away. They will remember thee,

By many a word of witness for the truth,
And many a deed of bounty. In the sphere
Of those sublimer charities that gird
The mind—the soul—thine was the ready hand;
And for the hasting of that day of peace
Which sheathes the sword, thine was the earnest
prayer.

In thine own house and in the church of God
There will be weeping for thee. Thou no more
Around thine altar shalt delight to see
Thy children, and thy children's children, come
To take thy patriarch blessing,—and no more
Bring duly to yon consecrated courts
Thy sabbath offering. Thou hast gained the
rest
Which earthly sabbaths dimly shadow forth,
And to that ransomed family art risen
Which have no need of prayer.
But thou, O man!
Whose hold on life is like the spider's web,
Who hast thy footing 'mid so many snares,
So many pitfalls, yet perceivest them not,—
Seek peace with Him who made thee,—bind
the shield
Of faith in Christ more firmly o'er thy breast,
That, when its pulse stands still, thy soul may
pass,
Unshrinking, unreluctant, unamazed,
Into the fulness of the light of Heaven.

PARTING HYMN OF MISSIONARIES TO BURMAH.

NATIVE Land! in summer smiling,—
  Hill and valley, grove and stream,—
Home! whose nameless charms beguiling
  Peaceful lull'd our infant dream,—
Haunts! thro' which our childhood hasted
  Where the earliest wild-flowers grew,
Church! where God's free grace we tasted,
  Gems on Memory's breast,—*adieu*.

Mother! who hast watch'd our pillow,
  In thy tender, sleepless love,—
Lo,—we dare the crested billow,—
  Mother!—put thy trust above;—
Father! from thy guidance turning,
  O'er the deep our way we take,—
Keep the prayerful incense burning
  On thine altar for our sake.

Brothers! sisters! more than ever
  Seem our clinging heart-strings twin'd,

As that hallow'd bond we sever
  Which the hand of nature join'd:
But the cry of pagan anguish
  Thro' our inmost hearts doth sound,
Countless souls in misery languish,
  We would haste to heal their wound.

Burmah! we would soothe thy weeping,
  Take us to thy sultry breast,
Where the sainted few are sleeping,
  Let us share a kindred rest:
Friends! our span of life is fleeting,
  Hark! the harps of angels swell,
Think of that eternal meeting
  Where no voice shall say farewell.

BABE BEREAVED OF ITS MOTHER

Fair is the tint of bloom,
  That decks thy brow, my child;
And bright thine eye looks forth from sleep,
  Still eloquent and mild;
But she, who would have joy'd
  Those opening charms to see,
And clasp'd thee in her sheltering arms
  With rapture—*where is she?*

To heed thine every want
  The watch of Love is near,
And all thy feeble plaints are heard
  With sympathy sincere;
Yet she, to whom that care
  Had been most deeply dear,
Who bare thee on her ceaseless prayer,
  The mother—is not here.

Soon will these lips of rose
  Their new-born speech essay,
But when thy little hopes and fears
  Win forth their lisping way,

The ear that would have lov'd
Their dove-like music best,
Lies mouldering in the lowly bed
Of death's unbroken rest.

Babe!—tho' thou may'st not call
Thy mother from the dead,
Yet canst thou learn the way she went,
And in her footsteps tread;
For sure that path will lead
Up to a glorious home,
Where happy spirits never part,
And evil cannot come.

Her's was the hope that glows
Unwavering and serene,
The chasten'd spirit's meek repose
In every changeful scene;
Her's was the victor-power
When mortal anguish came,—
Child!—be thy holy trust thro' life,
Thy peace in death, the same.

' WHITHER SHALL I FLEE FROM THY PRESENCE."—David.

Take morning's wing, and fly from zone to
zone,
To earth's remotest pole, and, ere old Time
Can shift one figure on his dial-plate,
Haste to the frigid Thule of mankind,
Where the scant life-drop freezes. Or go down
To Ocean's secret caverns, 'mid the throng
Of monsters without number, which no foot
Of man hath visited, and yet returned
To walk among the living. Or the shroud
Of midnight wrap around thee, dense and deep
Bidding thy spirit slumber.
Hop'st thou thus
To 'scape the Almighty, to whose piercing eye
Morn's robe and midnight's vestments are the
same?
Spirit of truth!—why should we seek to hide
Motive or deed from thee?—why strive to walk
In a vain show before our fellow-men?
Since at the same dread audit each must stand,

And with a sun-ray read his brother's breast
While his own thoughts are weighed?
Search thou my soul!
And, if aught evil lurks securely there
Like Achan's stolen hoard, command it thence,
And hold me up in singleness of heart,
And simple, child-like confidence in Thee,
Till time shall close his labyrinth, and ope
Eternity's broad gate.

THE INDIAN'S WELCOME TO THE PILGRIM FATHERS.

"On Friday, March 16th, 1622, while the colonists were busied in their usual labors, they were much surprised to see a savage walk boldly towards them, and salute them with, 'much welcome. English, much welcome, Englishmen.' "

Above them spread a stranger sky
  Around, the sterile plain,
The rock-bound coast rose frowning nigh,
  Beyond,—the wrathful main:
Chill remnants of the wintry snow
  Still chok'd the encumber'd soil,
Yet forth those Pilgrim Fathers go,
  To mark their future toil.

'Mid yonder vale their corn must rise
  In summer's ripening pride,
And there the church-spire woo the skies
  Its sister-school beside.

Perchance 'mid England's velvet green
 Some tender thought repos'd,—
Though nought upon their stoic mien
 Such soft regret disclos'd.

When sudden from the forest wide
 A red-brow'd chieftain came,
With towering form, and haughty stride,
 And eye like kindling flame:
No wrath he breath'd, no conflict sought,
 To no dark ambush drew,
But simply *to the Old World brought,*
 The welcome of the New.

That *welcome* was a blast and ban
 Upon thy race unborn.
Was there no seer, thou fated Man!
 Thy lavish zeal to warn?
Thou in thy fearless faith didst hail
 A weak, invading band,
But who shall heed thy children's wail
 Swept from their native land?

Thou gav'st the riches of thy streams,
 The lordship o'er thy waves,
The region of thine infant dreams,
 And of thy father's graves,
But who to yon proud mansions pil'd
 With wealth of earth and sea,
Poor outcast from thy forest wild,
 Say, who shall welcome thee?

BIRTH-DAY OF THE FIRST-BORN

THY first-born's birth-day, Mother!
  That well-remember'd time
Returneth, when thy heart's deep joy
  Swell'd to its highest prime.

Thou hast another treasure,
  There in the cradle-shrine,
And she who near its pillow plays,
  With cheek so fair, is thine.

But still, thy brow is shaded,
  The fresh tear trickleth free,
Where is that first-born darling?
  Young Mother, where is she?

And, if she be in heaven,
  She, who with goodness fraught,
So early on her Father-God
  Repos'd her trusting thought,

And, if she be in heaven,
  The honour how divine,
To yield an angel to his arms
  Who gave a babe to thine.

THE HALF-CENTURY SERMON.

LOOK back, look back, ye grey-hair'd worshippers,
Who to this hill-top *fifty years ago*
Came up with solemn joy. Withdraw the folds
Which curtaining time hath gather'd o'er the scene,
And show its colouring. The dark cloud of war
Faded to fitful sun-light,—on the ear,
The rumour of red battle died away,
And there was Peace in Zion. So a throng
O'er a faint carpet of the spring's first green
Were seen in glad procession hasting on,
To set a watchman on these sacred walls.
Each eye upon his consecrated brow
Was fondly fix'd, for in its pallid hue,
In its deep, thought-worn, spiritual lines,
They trac'd the mission of the crucified,
The hope of Israel. High the anthem swell'd,
Ascribing glory to the Lord of Hosts,
Who in his bounteous goodness thus vouchsaf'd
To beautify his temple.

The same strain
Riseth once more; but where are they who pour'd
Its tones melodious, on that festal day?
Young men and maidens of the tuneful lip,
The bright in beauty, and the proud in strength,
With bosoms fluttering to illusive hope,
Where are they? Can ye tell, ye hoary ones,
Who, few, and feebly leaning on the staff,
Bow down, where erst with manhood's lofty port
Ye tower'd as columns? They have sunk away,
Brethren and sisters, from your empty grasp,
Like bubbles on the pool, and ye are left,
With life's long lessons furrow'd on your brow.

Change worketh all around you. The lithe twig
That in your boyhood ye did idly bend
Maketh broad shadow, and the forest-king,
Arching majestic o'er your school-day sports,
Mouldereth, to sprout no more. The little babe
Ye as a plaything dandled, of whose frame
Perchance ye spake as most exceeding frail
And prone to perish like the flower of grass,
Doth nurse his children's children on his knee.

—But still your ancient shepherd's voice ye hear,

Tho' age hath quell'd its power, and well those tones
Of serious, saintly tenderness do stir
The springs of love and reverence. As your guide
He in the heavenward path hath firmly walk'd,
Bearing your joys and sorrows in his breast,
And on his prayers. He at your household hearths
Hath spoke his Master's message, while your babes,
Listening, imbibed as blossoms drink the dew;
And when your dead were buried from your sight,
Was he not there?
His scatter'd locks are white
With the hoar-frost of time, but in his soul
There is no winter. He, the uncounted gold
Of many a year's experience richly spreads
To a new generation, and methinks
With high prophetic brow doth stand sublime
Like Moses 'tween the living and the dead,
To make atonement. God's unclouded smile
Sustain thee, patriarch! like a flood of light
Still brightening, till, with those whom thou hast taught
And warn'd in wisdom, and with weeping love
Led to the brink of Calvary's cleansing stream,
Thou strike the victor harp o'er sin and death.

DEATH OF A BEAUTIFUL BOY.

I SAW thee at thy mother's side, when she was
marble cold,
And thou wert like some cherub form, cast in
ethereal mould;
But, when the sudden pang of grief oppressed
thine infant thought,
And 'mid thy clear and radiant eye a liquid
crystal wrought,
I thought how strong that faith must be that
breaks a mother's tie,
And bids her leave her darling's tears for other
hands to dry.

I saw thee in thine hour of sport, beside thy
father's bower,
Amid his broad and bright parterre, thyself the
fairest flower,
I heard thy tuneful voice ring out upon the
summer air,
As though some bird of Eden poured its joyous
carol there,

And lingered with delighted gaze on happy
childhood's charms,
Which once the blest Redeemer loved, and
folded in his arms.

I saw thee scan the classic page, with high and
glad surprise,
And saw the sun of science beam, as on an
eaglet's eyes,
And marked thy strong and brilliant mind
arouse to bold pursuit,
And from the tree of knowledge pluck its
richest, rarest fruit;
Yet still from such precocious power I shrank
with secret fear,
A shuddering presage that thy race must soon
be ended here.

I saw thee in the house of God, and loved the
reverent air
With which thy beauteous head was bowed low
in thy guileless prayer,
Yet little deemed how soon thy place would be
with that blest band
Who ever near the Eternal Throne, in sinless
worship, stand;
Ah, little deemed how soon the tomb must lock
thy glorious charms,
And wing thine ardent soul to find a sainted
mother's arms.

FOREIGN MISSIONS.

Up, at the Gospel's glorious call!
Country and kindred what are they?
Rend from thy heart, these charmers, *all*,
Christ needs thy service, hence away.

Tho' free the parting tear may rise,
Tho' high may roll the boisterous wave;
Go, find thy home 'neath foreign skies,
And shroud thee in a stranger's grave.

Perchance, the Hindoo's languid child,
The infant at the Burman's knee,
The shiverer in the arctic wild,
Shall bless the Eternal Sire for thee.

And what hath Earth compar'd to this?
Knows she of wealth or joy like thine?
The ransom'd heathen's heavenly bliss,
The plaudit of the Judge divine?

EVENING THOUGHTS.

Come to thy lonely bower, thou who dost love
The hour of musing. Come, before the brow
Of twilight darkens, or the solemn stars
Look from their casement. 'Mid that hush of soul,
Music from viewless harps shall visit thee,
Such as thou never heard'st amid the din
Of earth's coarse enginery, by toil and care
Urged on, without reprieve. Ah! kneel and catch
That tuneful cadence. It shall wing thy thought
Above the jarrings of this time-worn world,
And give the key-tone of that victor-song
Which plucks the sting from death.
How closely wrapt
In quiet slumber are all things around!
The vine-leaf and the willow-fringe stir not,
Nor doth the chirping of the feeblest bird,
Nor even the cold glance of the vestal moon,
Disturb thy reverie. Yet dost thou think
To be alone?—In fellowship more close

Than man with man, pure spirits hover near,
Prompting to high communion with the Source
Of every perfect gift. Lift up the soul,
For 'tis a holy pleasure thus to find
Its melody of musing so allied
To pure devotion. Give thy prayer a voice,
Claiming Heaven's blessing on these sacred
hours,
Which, in the world's warped balance weighed,
might yield
But sharp derision. Sure they help to weave
Such robes as angels wear; and thou shalt taste
In their dear, deep, entrancing solitude
Such sweet society, that thou shalt leave
"Signet and staff," as pledges of return.

THE AFRICAN MOTHER AT HER DAUGHTER'S GRAVE.

Some of the pagan Africans visit the burial-places of their departed relatives, bearing food and drink;—and mothers have been known, for a long course of years, to bring, in an agony of grief, their annual oblation to the tombs of their children

"Daughter! I bring thee food;
 The rice-cake, pure and white,
The cocoa, with its milky blood,
 Dates, and pomegranates bright,
The orange, in its gold,
 Fresh from thy favourite tree,
Nuts, in their ripe and husky fold,
 Dearest! I spread for thee.

"Year after year, I tread
 Thus to thy low retreat,—
But now the snow-hairs mark my head,
 And age enchains my feet.

O! many a change of woe
 Hath dimmed thy spot of birth,
Since first my gushing tears did flow
 O'er this thy bed of earth.

"There came a midnight cry;
 Flames from our hamlet rose;
A race of pale-browed men were nigh,—
 They were our country's foes:
Thy wounded sire was borne
 By tyrant force away
Thy brothers from our cabin torn,
 While in my blood I lay.

"I watched for their return,
 Upon the rocky shore,
Till night's red planets ceased to burn,
 And the long rains were o'er.
Till seeds, their hands had sown,
 A ripened fruitage bore,
The billows echoed to my moan,
 Yet they returned no more.

"But thou art slumbering deep,—
 And to my wildest cry,
When, pierced with agony, I weep,
 Dost render no reply.
Daughter! my youthful pride,
 The idol of my eye;—

Why didst thou leave thy mother's side,
  Beneath these sands to lie?"

Long o'er the hopeless grave
  Where her lost darling slept,
Invoking gods that could not save,
  That pagan mourner wept.
O! for some voice of power,
  To soothe her bursting sighs:—
"There is a resurrection hour;
  Thy daughter's dust shall rise!"

Christians! ye hear the cry
  From heathen Afric's strand,—
Haste! lift salvation's banner high
  O'er that benighted land:
With faith that claims the skies,
  Her misery control,
And plant the hope that never dies
  Deep in her tear-wet soul.

TO MOURNING PARENTS.

Tender guides, in sorrow weeping,
  O'er your first-born's smitten bloom,
Or fond memory's vigil keeping
  Where the fresh turf marks her tomb,

Ye no more shall see her bearing
  Pangs that woke the dove-like moan,
Still for your affliction caring,
  Though forgetful of her own.

Ere the bitter cup she tasted,
  Which the hand of care doth bring,
Ere the glittering pearls were wasted,
  From glad childhood's fairy string,

Ere one chain of hope had rusted,
  Ere one wreath of joy was dead,
To the Saviour, whom she trusted,
  Strong in faith, her spirit fled.

Gone—where no dark sin is cherished,
  Where no woes nor fears invade,
Gone—ere youth's first flower had perished,
  To a youth that ne'er can fade.

SAILOR'S FUNERAL.

THE ship's bell tolled, and slowly o'er the deck
Came forth the summoned crew.—Bold, hardy men,
Far from their native skies, stood silent there,
With melancholy brows. From a low cloud
That o'er the horizon hovered, came the threat
Of distant, muttered thunder. Broken waves
Heaved up their sharp white helmets o'er the expanse
Of ocean, which in brooding stillness lay,
Like some vindictive king who meditates
On hoarded wrongs, or wakes the wrathful war.

The ship's bell tolled!—And, lo, a youthful form
Which oft had boldly dared the slippery shrouds
At midnight watch, was as a burden laid
Down at his comrades' feet. Mournful they gazed
Upon his hollow cheek; and some there were
Who in that bitter hour remembered well
The parting blessing of his hoary sire,

And the fond tears that o'er his mother's cheek
Went coursing down, when his gay, happy voice
Left its farewell. But one who nearest stood
To that pale shrouded corse remembered more ;—
Of a white cottage with its shaven lawn,
And blossomed hedge, and of a fair-haired girl
Who, at a lattice veiled with woodbine, watched
His last far step, and then turned back to weep.
And close that comrade in his faithful breast
Hid a bright chesnut lock, which the dead youth
Had severed with a cold and trembling hand
In life's extremity, and bade him bear
With broken words of love's last eloquence
To his blest Mary. Now that chosen friend,
Bowed low his sun-burnt face, and like a child
Sobbed in deep sorrow.
But there came a tone
Clear as the breaking moon o'er stormy seas·
"I am the resurrection."—Every heart
Suppressed its grief, and every eye was raised.
There stood the chaplain, his uncovered brow
Unmarked by earthly passion, while his voice,
Rich as the balm from plants of paradise,
Poured the Eternal's message o'er the souls
Of dying men. It was a holy hour!

There was a plunge!—The riven sea complained,

Death from her briny bosom took his own.
The troubled fountains of the deep lift up
Their subterranean portals, and he went
Down to the floor of ocean, 'mid the beds
Of brave and beautiful ones. Yet to my soul,
'Mid all the funeral pomp with which this earth
Indulgeth her dead sons, was nought so sad,
Sublime, or sorrowful, as the mute sea
Opening her mouth to whelm that sailor youth.

CHRISTIAN HOPE.

"If ye then be risen with Christ, seek those things that are from above, where Christ sitteth on the right hand of God. Set your affections on things above; for ye are dead, and your life is hid with Christ in God."—St. Paul.

If with the Lord your hope doth rest,
With Christ who reigns above,
Loose from its bonds your captive breast,
And heavenward point its love.

Yes, heavenward. Ye're of holy birth,
Bid your affections soar
Above the vain delights of earth,
Which, fading, bloom no more.

Seek ye some pure and thornless rose?
Some friend with changeless eye?
Some fount whence living water flows?
Go, seek those things on high.

Thither bid Hope a pilgrim go,
  And Faith her mansion rear,
Even while amid this world of woe
  Ye shed the stranger's tear.

If folly tempts, or sin allures,
  Be deaf to all their art.
So, shall eternal life be yours
  When time's brief years depart.

LADY JANE GREY.

ON SEEING A PICTURE REPRESENTING HER ENGAGED IN THE STUDY OF PLATO.

So early wise! Beauty hath been to thee
No traitor-friend to steal the key
Of knowledge from thy mind,
Making thee gorgeous to the eye,
Flaunting and flushed with vanity,
Yet inly blind.

Hark! the hunting-bugle sounds,
Thy father's park is gay,
Stately nobles cheer the hounds,
Soft hands the coursers sway,
Haste to the sport, away! away!
Youth, and mirth, and love, are there,
Lingerest thou, fairest of the fair,
In thy lone chamber to explore
Ancient Plato's classic lore?

Grave Roger Ascham's gaze
Is fix'd on thee with fond amaze;

Doubtless the sage doth marvel deep,
That, for philosophy divine,
A lady could decline
The pleasure 'mid yon pageant-train to sweep,
The glory o'er some five-barr'd gate to leap,
And, in the toil of reading Greek,
Which many a student flies,
Find more entrancing rhetoric
Than fashion's page supplies.

Ah, sweet enthusiast! happier far for thee
Had'st thou thy musing intellectual joy
Thro' life indulg'd without alloy,
In solitary sanctity,—
Nor dar'd ambition's fearful shrift,
Nor laid thy shrinking hand on Edward's fatal
gift.

The crown! the crown! It sparkles on thy
brow,
I see Northumberland with joy elate,
And low thy haughty sire doth bow,
Honouring thy high estate,
She, too, the austerely beautiful, whose eye
Check'd thy timid infancy,
Until thy heart's first buds folded their leaves to
die,
Homage to her meek daughter pays:
Yet, sooth to say, one fond embrace,
One kiss, such as the peasant-mother gives

When on its evening bed her child she lays,
Had dearer been to thee, than all their courtly
phrase.

The tower! the tower! thou bright-hair'd beau
teous one!
There, where the captive's breath
Hath sigh'd itself in bitterness away,
Where iron nerves have withered one by one,
And the sick eye, shut from the glorious sun,
Grop'd mid those chilling walls till idiocy
Made life like death,—
There must thy resting be?

Not long. Not long! What savage band
'Neath thy grated window bears
His headless form, his lifeless hand
The magic of whose love could charm
away thy cares?
Guildford! thy husband! yet the gushing tear
Scarce flows to mourn his fate severe,
Thy pious thought doth rise
To those unclouded skies,
Where he, amid the angel train,
Doth for thy coming wait, to part no more again.

The scaffold! Must it be!—Stern England's
Queen,
Hast thou such doom decreed?
Dwells Draco's soul beneath a woman's mein?

Must guileless youth and peerless beauty
bleed?
Away! Away! I will not see the deed.
Fresh drops of crimson stain the new-fall'n
snow,
The wintry winds wail fitfully and low;—
But the meek victim is not there,
Far from this troubled scene,
High o'er the tyrant queen,
She finds that crown which from her brow
No envious hand may tear.

DEATH OF A MISSIONARY IN AFRICA.

THERE is a sigh from Niger's sable realm,
A voice of Afric's weeping. One hath fallen,
Who, with the fervour of unresting love,
Allur'd her children to a Saviour's arms.

Alone he fell,—that heart so richly fill'd
With all affection's brightest imagery,
In its drear stranger-solitude endured
The long death-struggle, and sank down to rest.

Say ye, alone he fell? It was not so,
There was a hovering of celestial wings
Around his lowly couch, a solemn sound
Of stricken harps, such as around God's throne
Make music night and day. He might not tell
Of that high music, for his lips were sealed,
And his eye closed. And so, ye say,—*he died?*
But all the glorious company of heaven
Do say,—*he lives*, and that your brief farewell,
Uttered in tears, was but the prelude tone
Of the full welcome of eternity.

DIRGE.

"Mourn for the *living*, and not for the *dead*."
HEBREW DIRGE

I SAW an infant, marble cold,
  Borne from the pillowing breast,
And, in the shroud's embracing fold,
  Laid down to dreamless rest;
And, moved with bitterness, I sighed,—
  Not for the babe that slept,
But for the mother at its side,
  Whose soul in anguish wept.

They bore a coffin to its place,
  I asked them, "Who was there?"
And they replied, "A form of grace;
  The fairest of the fair."
But for that blest one do ye moan,
  Whose angel-wing is spread?
No; for the lover, pale and lone,—
  His heart is with the dead.

I wandered to a new-made grave,
  And there a matron lay,—
The love of Him who died to save,
  Had been her spirit's stay.
Yet sobs burst forth of torturing pain;—
  Wail ye for her who died?
No; for that timid, infant train,
  Who roam without a guide.

Why should we mourn for those who die,—
  Whose rise to glory's sphere?
The tenants of that cloudless sky
  Need not our mortal tear.
Our woe seems arrogant and vain;
  Perchance it moves their scorn,
As if the slave, beneath his chain,
  Deplored the princely born.

We live to meet a thousand foes;
  We shrink with bleeding breast,—
Why should we weakly mourn for those
  Who dwell in perfect rest?
Bound, for a few sad, fleeting years,
  A thorn-clad path to tread,
O! for the living spare those tears
  Ye lavish on the dead.

VÆ VOBIS.*

"*Væ Vobis*," ye whose lip doth lave
So deeply in the sparkling wine,
Regardless though that passion-wave
Shut from the soul, Heaven's light divine,
"*Væ Vobis*,"—heed the trumpet-blast,
Fly !—ere the leprous taint is deep,
Fly !—ere the hour of hope be past,
And pitying angels cease to weep.

"*Væ Vobis*,"—ye who fail to read
The name that shines where'er ye tread,
The Alpha of our infant creed,
The Omega of the sainted dead:
It glows where'er the pencil'd flowers
Their tablet to the desert show,
Where'er the mountain's rocky towers
Frown darkly o'er the vale below:

Where roll the wondrous orbs on high
In glorious order, strong and fair,

* "Woe unto you."

In every letter of the sky
  That midnight writes,—'tis there! 'tis there!
'Tis grav'd on ocean's wrinkled brow,
  And on the shell that gems its shore,
And where the solemn forests bow,
  "*Væ Vobis*," ye, who scorn the lore.

"*Væ Vobis*" all who trust in earth,
  Who lean on reeds that pierce the breast,
Who toss the bubble-cup of mirth,
  Or grasp ambition's storm-wreath'd crest;
Who early rise, and late take rest,
  In Mammon's mine, the care-worn slave,
Who find each phantom-race unblest,
  Yet shrink reluctant from the grave.

BOY'S LAST BEQUEST.

HALF-RAISED upon his dying couch, his head
Drooped o'er his mother's bosom,—like a bud
Which, broken from its parent stalk, adheres
By some attenuate fibre. His thin hand
From 'neath the downy pillow drew a book,
And slowly pressed it to his bloodless lip.

"Mother, dear mother, see your birth-day gift,
Fresh and unsoiled. Yet have I kept your word,
And ere I slept each night, and every morn,
Did read its pages, with my humble prayer,
Until this sickness came."
He paused—for breath
Came scantily, and with a toilsome strife.
"Brother or sister have I none, or else
I'd lay this Bible on their hearts, and say,
Come, read it on my grave, among the flowers:
So you who gave it must take it back again,
And love it for my sake." "My son!—my son,"

Murmured the mourner, in that tender tone
Which woman, in her sternest agony
Commands, to soothe the pang of those she loves,
"The soul! the soul!—to whose charge yield you that?"
"Mother,—to God who gave it."
So, that soul
With a slight shudder and a lingering smile
Left the pale clay for its Creator's arms.

"HINDER THEM NOT."

"'Suffer little children to come unto me, and forbid them not.' But you hinder them by your example, and by not encouraging them. Their course ought to be upward:—do not hinder them."
REV MR. TAYLOR, *of the Seamen's Chapel, Boston*

LOCK'D in the bosom of the earth
  The little seed its heart doth stir,
And quickening for its mystic birth,
  Burst from its cleaving sepulchre,
The aspiring head, the unfolding leaf,
  Exulting in their joyous lot,
Turn grateful towards the Eye of Day,
  Hinder them not.

Thus, do the buds of being rise
  From cradle-dreams, like snow-drop meek,
While through their mind-illumin'd eyes
  A deathless principle doth speak,

Already toward a brighter sphere
  They turn, from this terrestrial spot,—
Fond parents!—florists kind and dear!
  Hinder them not.

Hinder them not!—even Love may spare
  In blindness many a wayward shoot,—
Or weakly let the usurping tare
  Divert the health-stream from their root;
Oh! by that negligence supine,
  Which oft the fairest page doth blot,
And shroud the ray of light divine,
  Hinder them not.

Cold world!—the teachings of thy guile
  Awhile from these young hearts restrain;
Oh spare that unsuspicious smile
  Which never must return again;
By folly's wile, by falsehood's kiss
  Too soon acquir'd, too late forgot,
By sins that shut the soul from bliss
  Hinder them not.

MORAVIAN MISSIONS TO GREEN LAND.

WHY steers yon bold adventurous prow
 On toward the arctic zone,
Defying blasts that rudely seal
 To Ocean's breast like stone?
Why dare her crew those fearful seas
 Where icy mountains dash,
And make the proudest ship a wreck
 With one tremendous crash?

They come, who seek the spirit's gold
 They dare yon dreary sphere,
And winter startles on his throne,
 Their strain of praise to hear:
They come, Salvation's lamp to light
 Where frost and darkness reign,
And with a deathles joy to cheer
 The sons of want and pain.

And lo! the chapel rears its head
 Beneath those stranger-skies,

And to the sweet-ton'd Sabbath-bell
  The thick-ribb'd ice replies.
The unletter'd Esquimaux doth pluck
  The victory from the tomb,
And grateful seek that glorious clime
  Where flowers forever bloom.

When the last tinge of green departs,
  The last bird takes its flight,
And the far sun no beam bestows
  On that long polar night,
When in her subterranean cell
  To shun the tempest's ire,
Life shrinking guards her pallid flame
  That feebly lifts its spire,

The teachers of a love divine,
  That firm, devoted band,
With no weak sigh of fond regret
  Recall their father-land,
The unchanging smile that lights their brow,
  While storms of Winter roar,
Doth better prove their heaven-born Faith
  Than Learning's loftiest lore.

PAUL AT ATHENS.

Come to the hill of Mars—for he is there
That wondrous man whose eloquence doth touch
The heart like living flame. With brow unblanched
And eye of fearless ardour, he confronts,
That high tribunal with its pen of flint,
Whose irreversible decree, made pale
The Gentile world. All Athens gathers near,
Fickle, and warm of heart, and fond of change
And full of strangers, and of those who pass
Life in the idle toil to hear, or tell,
Of some new thing. See, thither throng the bands
Of Epicurus, wrapt in gorgeous robe,
Who seem with bright and eager eyes to ask
"What will this babbler say?"—With front austere,
Stand a dark group of Stoics, sternly proud—
And predetermined to confute; yet still
'Neath the deep wrinkles of their settled brow

Lurks some unwonted gathering of their powers
As for no common foe. With angry frown
Stalk the fierce Cynics, anxious to condemn,
And prompt to punish, while the patient sons
Of gentle Plato bow the listening soul
To search for wisdom, and with reason's art
Build the fair argument. Behold the throngs
Press on the speaker, drawing still more close
In denser circles, as his thrilling tones
Teach of the God who "warneth everywhere
Men to repent," and of that fearful day
When He shall judge the world. Loud tumult
wakes,
The tide of strong emotion hoarsely swells,
And that blest voice is silent. They have
mocked
At Heaven's high messenger, and he departs
From the mad circle. But his graceful hand
Points to an altar, with its mystic scroll—
"The Unknown God."—Oh! Athens! is it so?
Thou who hast crowned thyself with woven
rays
As a divinity, and called the world
Thy pilgrim-worshipper, dost thou confess
Such ignorance and shame?
The Unknown God!
Why, all thy hillocks and resounding streams
Do boast their deity, and every house,
Yea, every beating heart within thy walls,
May choose its temple and its priestly train,

Victim and garland, and appointed rite;
Thou makest the gods of every realm thine own,
Fostering, with frantic hospitality,
All forms of idol-worship. Can i. be
That still thou found'st not Him who is so near
To every one of us, in "whom we live,
And move, and have our being?" Found not Him
Of whom thy poets spake with childlike awe?

And thou, philosophy, whose art, refined,
Did aim to pierce the labyrinth of fate,
And compass with a fine-spun sophist web
This mighty universe—didst thou fall short
Of the Upholding Cause?—
The Unknown God?
Thou who didst smile to find the admiring world
Crouch as a pupil to thee, wert thou blind?—
Blinder than he who, in his humble cot,
With hardened hand, his daily labour done,
Turneth the page of Jesus and doth read,
With toil, perchance, that the trim schoolboy scorns,
Counting him, in his arrogance, a fool?
Yet shall the poor, wayfaring man lie down
With such a hope as thou could'st never teach
Thy king-like sages—yea, a hope that plucks
The sting from death, the victory from the grave

THE MUFFLED KNOCKER.

GRIEF! Grief! 'tis thy symbol, so mute and
dread,
Yet it hath a tale for the listening ear,
Of the nurse's care, and the curtain'd bed,
Of the baffled healer's cautious tread;
And the midnight lamp, with its flickering ligh
Half screen'd from the restless sufferer's sight;
Yes, many a sable scene of woe,
Doth that muffled knocker's tablet show.

Pain! Pain! art thou wrestling here with man;
For the broken gold of his wasted span?
Art thou straining thy rack on his tortur'd nerve
Till his firmest hopes from their anchor swerve?
Till burning tears from his eye-balls flow,
And his manhood faints in a shriek of woe?
Methinks, thy scorpion-sting I trace,
Through the mist of that sullen knocker's face.

Death! Death! do I see thee with weapon
dread,
Art thou laying thy hand on yon cradle bed?

The mother is there, with her sleepless eye,
To dispute each step of thy victory.
She doth fold the child in her soul's embrace,
Her prayer is, to die in her idol's place,
She hath bared her breast to thine arrow's sway,
But thou will not be bribed from that babe
away.

Earth! Earth! thou hast stamp'd on thy scroll
of bliss
The faithless seal of a traitor's kiss,
Where the bridal lamp gleam'd clear and bright,
And the foot through the maze of the dance was
light,
Thou biddest the black-robed weeper kneel,
And the heavy hearse roll its lumbering wheel,
And still to the heart that will heed its lore,
Does Wisdom speak from yon muffled door.

CHANGES.

THE vines are wither'd, O, my love,
  That erst we taught to tower,
And in a mesh of fragrance wove,
  Around our summer-bower.

The ivy on the ancient wall
  Doth in its budding fade;
The stream is dry, whose gentle fall
  A lulling murmur made.

The tangled weeds have chok'd the flowers
  The trees, so lately bright,
In all the pomp of vernal hours
  Reveal a blackening blight;

There is a sigh upon the gale
  That doth the willow sway,
A murmur from the blossoms pale,
  "Arise, and come away."

So, when this life in clouds shall hide
  Its garland fair and brief,

And every promise of its pride
  Must wear the frosted leaf;

Then may the undying soul attain
  That heritage sublime,
Where comes no pang of parting pain,
  Nor change of hoary time.

ON READING THE MEMOIRS OF MRS. JUDSON.

I SAW her on the strand. Beside her smil d
The land of birth, and the beloved home,
With all their pageantry of tint and shade,
Streamlet and vale.
 There stood her childhood's friends,
Sweet sisters, who her inmost thoughts had shar'd,
And saint-like parents, whose example rais'd
Those thoughts to heaven. It was a strong array,
And the fond heart clung to its rooted loves.
But Christ had given a panoply, which earth
Might never take away. And so she turn'd
To boisterous ocean, and with cheerful step,
Though moisten'd eye, forsook the cherish'd clime
Whose halcyon bowers had rear'd her joyous youth.
—I look'd again. It was a foreign shore.
The tropic sun had laid his burning brow

On twilight's lap. A gorgeous palace caught
His last red ray. Hoarsely the idol-song
To Boodh mingled with the breeze that curl'd
Broad Irrawaddy's tide. Why do ye point
To yon low prison? Who is he that gropes
Amid its darkness, with those fetter'd limbs?
Mad Pagans! do ye *thus* requite the man
Who toils for your salvation?
See that form
Bending in tenderest sympathy to soothe
The victim's sorrow. Tardy months pass by,
And find her still intrepid at the post
Of danger and of disappointed hope.
Stern sickness smote her, yet, with tireless zeal,
She bore the hoarded morsel to her love,
Dar'd the rude arrogance of savage power,
To plead for him, and bade his dungeon glow,
With her fair brow, as erst the angel's smile
Arous'd imprison'd Peter, when his hands,
From fetters loos'd, were lifted high in praise.

—There was another scene, drawn by his hand
Whose icy pencil blotteth out the grace
And loveliness of man. The keenest shaft
Of anguish quivers in that martyr's breast,
Who is about to wash her garments white
In a Redeemer's blood, and glorious rise
From earthly sorrows to a clime of rest.
—Dark Burman faces are around her bed,

And one pale babe is there, for whom she checks
The death-groan, clasping it in close embrace,
Even till the heart-strings break.
Behold he comes
The wearied man of God from distant toil.
His home, while yet a misty speck it seems,
His straining eye detects, but marks no form
Of his most lov'd one, hasting down the vale
As wont, to meet him.
Say, what heathen lip
In its strange accents told him, that on earth
Nought now remain'd to heal his wounded heart,
Save that lone famish'd infant? Days of care,
Were meted to him, and long nights of grief
Weigh'd out, and then that little, wailing one,
Went to her mother's bosom, and slept sweet
'Neath the cool branches of the hopia-tree.
'Twas bitterness to think that bird-like voice,
Which sang sweet hymns to please a father's ear,
Must breathe no more.
This is to be alone,
Alone in this wide world.
Yet not without
A comforter. For the true heart that trusts
Its all to Heaven, and sees its treasur'd things
Unfold their hidden wing, and thither soar,
Doth find itself drawn upward in their flight.

TRIBUTE
TO THE REV. DR. CORNELIUS.

"All ye that were about him, bemoan him, and all ye that know his name, say, how is the strong staff broken,—and the beautiful rod?"—THE PROPHET JEREMIAH.

AND can it be,—and *can it be,* that thou art on
thy bier?
But yesterday in all the prime of life's unspent
career!
I've seen the forest's noblest tree laid low, when
lightnings shine,
The column in its majesty torn from the temple-
shrine,
Yet little deem'd that ice so soon would check
thy vital stream,
Or the sun that soar'd without a cloud thus veil
its noon day beam.

I've seen thee in thy glory stand, while all
around was hush'd,
And seraph-wisdom from thy lips in tones of
music gush'd,
For thou with willing hand didst lay, at morn
ing's dewy hour,
Upon the altar of thy God thy beauty and thy
power,
Thou, for the helpless sons of woe, didst plead
with words of flame,
And boldly strike the rocky heart in thy Re-
deemer's name.

And, lo! that withering race who fade as dew
'neath summer's ray,
Who, like uprooted weeds, are cast from their
own earth away,
Who trusted to a nation's vow, yet found that
faith was vain,
And to their fathers' sepulchres return no more
again;
They need thy blended eloquence of lip, and
eye, and brow,
They need the righteous for a shield; *why art
thou absent now?*

Long shall thine image freshly dwell beside their
native streams,
And, 'mid their wanderings far and wide, illume
their alien dreams.

For Heaven to their sequester'd haunts thine
early steps did guide,
And the Cherokee hath heard thy prayer his
cabin-hearth beside,
The Osage orphan sadly breath'd her sorrows
to thine ear,
And the stern warrior knelt him down with
strange repentant tear.

I see a consecrated throng of youthful watchmen
rise,
Each girding on for Zion's sake their heaven-
wrought panoplies;
These, in their solitudes obscure, thy generous
ardour sought,
And gathering with a tireless hand, up to the
temple brought,
These, while the altar of their God they serve
with hallow'd zeal,
Shall wear thy memory on their heart, an ever-
lasting seal.

I hear a voice of wailing from the islands of the
sea,
Salvation's distant heralds mourn on heathen
shores for thee;
Thy constant love, like Gilead's balm refresh'd
their weary mind,
And with the blessed Evart's name thine own
was strongly twin'd,

But thou, from this illusive scene, hast like a vision fled,
Just wrapp'd his mantle o'er thy breast, then join'd him with the dead.

Farewell! we yield thee to the tomb, with many a bitter tear,
Tho' 'twas not meet a soul like thine should longer tarry here,
Fond, clustering hopes have sunk with thee, that earth can ne'er restore,
Love casts a garland on thy turf, that may not blossom more;
But thou art where each dream of hope shall in fruition fade,
And love, immortal and refin'd, glow on with out a shade.

CHARITY HYMN.

Widow! long estrang'd from gladness,
In thy cell so lonely made,
Where chill Penury's cloud of sadness
Adds to grief a sterner shade,
Look! the searching eye hath found thee;
Pitying hearts confess thy claim,
Bounteous spirits shed around thee
Blessings in a Saviour's name.

Orphan! in dependence weeping,
Crush'd by want and misery dire,
Or on lowly pallet sleeping,
Dreaming of thy buried sire,
Hands like his, combine to rear thee,
Stranger-arms are round thee cast,
And a Father ever near thee,
Fits the shorn lamb to the blast.

Brethren! by the precious token
Which the sons of mercy wear,
By the vows we here have spoken,
Grav'd in truth, and seal'd with prayer,

Penury's pathway we will brighten,
Misery with compassion meet,
And the heart of sorrow lighten,
Till our own shall cease to beat.

PICTURE OF A SLEEPING INFANT WATCHED BY A DOG.

Sweet are thy slumbers, baby. Gentle gales
Do lift the curtaining foliage o'er thy head,
And nested birds sing lullaby; and flowers
That form the living broidery of thy couch
Shed fresh perfume.
He, too, whose guardian eye
Pondereth thy features with such true delight,
And faithful semblance of parental care,
Counting his master's darling as his own
Should aught upon thy helpless rest intrude,
Would show a lion's wrath.
And when she comes,
Thy peasant-mother, from her weary toil,
Thy shout will cheer her, and thy little arms
Entwine her sunburnt neck, with joy as full
As infancy can feel. They who recline
In luxury's proud cradle, lulled with strains
Of warbling lute, and watched by hireling eyes,
And wrapt in golden tissue, share, perchance,
No sleep so sweet as thine.

Is it not thus
With us, the larger children? Gorgeous robes,
And all the proud appliances of wealth,
Touch not the heart's content; but he is blest,
Though clad in humble garb, who peaceful greets
The smile of nature, with a soul of love.

ON RETURNING FROM CHURCH.

The listening ear the hallow'd strain
  Has caught from lips devoutly wise,
But what my heart has been *thy* gain
  From all these precepts of the skies?

Contrition's lesson have they taught?
  The oft-forgotten vow renew'd?
Or gently touch'd thy glowing thought
  With the blest warmth of gratitude?

Say, from the low delights of time
  Thy best affections have they won?
Inciting thee with zeal sublime
  Earth's fleeting pilgrimage to run?

If not, how vain the band to join
  Who toward the house of God repair,
To pour the song of praise divine
  Or kneel in pharasaic prayer;

And ah! how vain when Death's cold hand
  Shall sternly reap time's ripen'd field,
How *worse than vain* when all must stand
  The last the dread account to yield.

THE BAPTISM.

'Twas near the close of that blest day, when, with melodious swell,
To crowded mart and lonely vale, had spoke the sabbath bell,
While on a broad, unruffled stream, with fringed verdure bright,
The westering sunbeam richly shed a tinge of crimson light.

When, lo! a solemn train appeared, by their loved pastor led,
And sweetly rose the holy hymn, as toward that stream they sped;
And he its cleaving, crystal breast, with graceful movement trod,
His steadfast eye upraised, to seek communion with its God.

Then, bending o'er his staff, approached that willow-shaded shore,
A man of many weary years, with furrowed temples hoar;

And faintly breathed his trembling lip—"Behold, I fain would be
Buried in baptism with my Lord, ere death should summon me."

With brow benign, like Him whose hand did wavering Peter guide,
The pastor bore his tottering frame through that translucent tide,
And plunged him 'neath the shrouding wave, and spake the Triune name,
And joy upon that withered face, in wondering radiance came.

And then advanced a lordly form, in manhood's towering pride,
Who from the gilded snares of earth had wisely turned aside,
And, following in His steps who bowed to Jordan's startled wave,
In deep humility of soul, this faithful witness gave.

Who next?—A fair and fragile form, in snowy robe doth move,
That tender beauty in her eye that wakes the vow of love—
Yea come, thou gentle one, and arm thy soul with strength divine,
This stern world hath a thousand darts to vex a breast like thine.

Beneath its smile a traitor's kiss is oft in darkness bound—
Cling to that Comforter who holds a balm for every wound;
Propitiate that Protector's care who never will forsake,
And thou shalt strike the harp of praise, even when thy heart-strings break.

Then, with a firm, unshrinking step, the watery path she trod,
And gave, with woman's deathless trust, her being to her God;
And when all drooping from the flood she rose, like lily-stem,
Methought that spotless brow might wear an angel's diadem.

Yet more! Yet more!—How meek they bow to their Redeemer's rite,
Then pass with music on their way, like joyous sons of light;
Yet lingering on those shores I staid, till every sound was hush'd,
For hallow'd musings o'er my soul, like spring-swollen rivers rush'd.

Tis better, said the voice within, to bear a Christian's cross,
Than sell this fleeting life for gold, which death shall prove but dross.

Far better when yon shrivell'd skies are like a
banner furl'd,
To share in Christ's reproach, than gain the
glory of the world.

DEATH OF THE WIFE OF A CLERGYMAN

DURING THE SICKNESS OF HER HUSBAND.

Dark sorrow brooded o'er the pastor's home,
The prayer was silent, and the loving group
That sang their hymn of praise at even and
morn
Now droop'd in pain,—or with a noiseless step
Tended the sick. It was a time of woe:
Days measur'd out in anguish, and drear nights
Mocking the eye that waited for the dawn.

They who from youth, by hallow'd vows con
join'd,
Had borne life's burdens with united arm,
And, side by side, its adverse fortunes foil'd
Apart,—an agonizing warfare wag'd
With nature's stern destroyer. Tidings pass'd
From couch to couch,—how stood the doubtful
strife
Twixt life and death. They might not lay their
hand

Upon each other's throbbing brow,—or breathe
The words of comfort, for disease had set
A gulf between them.
Hark! what sound appall'd
The suffering husband? 'Twas a mourner's sob
Beside his bed.
"My mother will not speak.—
They say she's *dead.*"—
Art thou the messenger,
Poor, pallid boy, that the dear love which sooth'd
The cradle-moan, and on thro' all thy life
Would still have clung to thee, untir'd, unchang'd,—
Is blotted out for ever?—Thou dost tell
A loss thou can'st not measure.
She,—the friend,—
The mother, imag'd in those daughters' hearts
First,—dearest,—best-belov'd,—who joy'd to walk
The meek companion of a man of God,—
Hath given her hand to that destroyer's grasp
Who rifleth the clay-cottage,—sending forth
The immortal habitant. Fearless, she laid
Earth's vestments by.
And thou, whose tenderest trust
With an unwonted confidence was seal'd
In that cold breast so long,—lift up thy soul.
'She is not here,—but risen!"—Shew the faith

Which thou hast preach'd to others,—by its power
In the dark night of trouble. Take the cross,—
And from thy stricken heart pour freshly forth
The spirit of thy Lord,—teaching thy flock
To learn Jehovah's lessons,—and be still.

CHRISTMAS HYMN.

Thou who, once an infant stranger,
  Honour'd this auspicious morn,
Thou who, in Judea's manger,
  Wert this day of woman born.

Thou whom wondering sages offer'd
  Costly gifts, and incense sweet,
Take our homage, humbly proffer'd,
  Grateful kneeling at thy feet.

Thou whose path a star of glory
  Gladly hasted to reveal
Herald of salvation's story,
  Touch our hearts with equal zeal:

Thou at whose approach was given
  Welcome from the angels' lyre,
Teach our souls the song of heaven,
  Ere we join their tuneful choir.

DEATH OF THE REV. GORDON HALL

The healer droops,—no more his skill
  May ease the sufferer's moan,—
The hand that sooth'd another's pang
  Sinks powerless 'neath its own;
The teacher dies;—he came to plant
  Deep in a heathen soil,
The germ of everlasting life,
  He faints amid the toil.

There was a vision of the Sea,
  That pain'd his dying strife,
Why stole that vision o'er his soul
  Thus 'mid the wreck of life?
A form, by holiest love endear'd,
  There rode the billowy crest,
And tenderly his pallid boys
  Were folded to her breast.

Then rose the long remember'd scenes
  Of his far, native bowers,
The white-spir'd church, the mother's hymn
  And boyhood's clustering flowers,

And strong that country of his heart,
  The green and glorious West,
Shar'd in the parting throb of love
  That shook the dying breast.

Brief was the thought, the dream, the pang,
  For high Devotion came,
And brought the martyr's speechless joy,
  And wing'd the prayer of flame,
And stamp'd upon the marble face
  Heaven's smile serenely sweet,
And bade the icy, quivering lip
  The praise of God repeat.

Strange, olive brows with tears were wet,
  As a lone grave was made,
And there, 'mid Asia's arid sands
  Salvation's herald laid,
But bright that shroudless clay shall burst
  From its uncoffin'd bed,
When the Archangel's awful trump
  Convenes the righteous dead.

TOMB OF ABSALOM.

Is this thy tomb, amid the mournful shades
Of the deep valley of Jehoshaphat,
Thou son of David? Kidron's gentle brook
Is murmuring near, as if it fain would tell
Thy varied history. Methinks I see
Thy graceful form, thy smile, thy sparkling eye,
The glorious beauty of thy flowing hair,
And that bright eloquent lip whose cunning stole
The hearts of all the people. Didst thou waste
The untold treasures of integrity,
The gold of conscience, for their light applause,
Thou fair dissembler?
Say, rememberest thou
When o'er yon flinty steep of Olive[illegible]
A sorrowing train went up? Dar[illegible]wning seers.
Denouncing judgment on a rebel prince,
Pass'd sadly on; and next a crownless king,
Walking in sad and humbled majesty,
While hoary statesmen bent upon his brow
Indignant looks of tearful sympathy —
What caused the weeping there?

Thou heard'st it not;
For thou within the city's walls didst hold
Thy revel, brief and base. And could'st thou
The embattled host against thy father's life,
The king of Israel, and the lov'd of God?
He, 'mid the evils of his changeful lot,
Saul's moody hatred, stern Philistia's spear,
His alien wanderings, and his warrior toil,
Found nought so bitter as the rankling thorn
Set, by thy madness of ingratitude,
Deep in his yearning soul.
What were thy thoughts
When in the mesh of thine own tresses snared
Amid the oak whose quiet verdure mocked
Thy misery? Wert thou forsook by all
Who shared thy meteor-greatness, and constrained
To learn, in that strange solitude of agony,
A traitor hath no friends?—What were thy thoughts
When death, careering on the triple dart
Of vengeful Joab, found thee? To thy God
Rose there one cry of penitence, one prayer
For that unmeasured mercy which can cleanse
Unbounded guilt? Or turned thy stricken heart
Toward him who o'er thy infant graces watched
With tender pride, and all thy sins of youth
In blindfold fondness pardoned?
Hark!—the breeze
That sweeps the palm-groves of Jerusalem

Bears the continuous wail, "O Absalom!—
My son!— my son!"—
We turn us from thy tomb,—
Usurping prince!—thy beauty and thy grace
Have perish'd with thee!—but thy fame survives,—
The ingrate son that pierc'd a father's heart.

DEATH OF A YOUNG LADY AT THE RETREAT FOR THE INSANE.

YOUTH glows upon her blossom'd cheek,
  Glad beauty in her eye,
And fond affections pure and meek
  Her every want supply:
Why doth her glance so wildly rove
  Some fancied foe to find?
What dark dregs stir her cup of love?
  Go ask the sickening mind!

They bear her where with cheering smile
  The hope of healing reigns
For those whom morbid Fancy's wile
  In torturing bond constrains;
Where Mercy spreads an angel-wing
  To do her Father's will,
And heaven-instructed, plucks the sting
  From earth's severest ill.

Yet o'er that sufferer's drooping head
  No balm of Gilead stole,

Diseas'd Imagination spread
  Dark chaos o'er the soul;
Tho' recollected truths sublime
  Still fed Devotion's stream,
And beings from a sinless clime
  Blent with her broken dream.

Then came a coffin and a shroud,
  And many a bursting sigh
With shrieks of laughter long and loud,
  From those who knew not why;
For she, whom Reason's fickle ray
  Oft wilder'd and distress'd
Hush'd in unwonted slumber lay,
  A cold and dreamless rest.

Think ye of Heaven! how glorious bright
  Will break its vision clear,
On souls that rose from earthly night
  All desolate and drear;
So ye who laid that stricken form
  Down to its willing sleep,
Snatch'd like a flowret from the storm,
  Weep not as others weep.

THE TOWER AT MONTEVIDEO.

Written after visiting the beautiful summer residence of DANIEL WADSWORTH, Esq., on Talcot mountain, near Hartford, Conn., which bears the name of Montevideo.

FULL many a year hath past away,
Thou rude, old Tower, so stern and grey,
Since first I came, enthusiast lone,
To worship at thy hermit throne.
—Tho' wintry blast, and sweeping rain
Have mark'd thee with their iron stain,
Yet freely springing at thy feet,
New beauties wreathe their garland sweet.
Young flowers the ancient wilds perfume,
In tangled dells, fresh roses bloom,
And foliage wraps with mantle deep.
The trap-rock ledges harsh and steep.
—Still spreads the lake its mirror clear,
The forest-warblers charm the ear,
The glorious prospect opens wide

Its varied page in summer's pride,
And tasteful hands have deftly wove
Enchantment's spell o'er vale and grove
Farewell old Tower! thou still shalt be
Remember'd as a friend by me,
Who bring'st from time's recorded track
The buds of joy profusely back,
And sweetly from thy turrets hoar
The song of gratitude dost pour,
Nor spare around my path to fling,
Young memory's brightest blossoming.
—When next we meet, perchance, the trace
Of age shall tint thy tottering base,
And I, with added plainness show
The wrinkled lines that care bestow;
But Nature still serene and fair,
No thread of silver in her hair,
No furrow'd mark on brow or cheek,
The same rich dialect shall speak,
With silent finger upward pointing,
And forehead pure with Heaven's anointing
And smile more eloquent than speech,
The lessons of her Sire shall teach.

BIRTH-DAY VERSES TO A LITTLE GIRL.

I do bethink me of a feeble babe,
To whom the gift of life did seem a toil
It trembled to take up, and of the care
That tireless nurtur'd her by night and day,
When it would seem as if the fainting breath
Must leave her bosom, and her fair blue eye
Sank 'neath its lids, like some crushed violet.
—Six winters came, and now that self-same babe
Wins with her needle the appointed length
Of her light task, and learns with patient zeal
The daily lesson, tracing on her map
All climes and regions of the peopled earth.
With tiny hand, she guides the writer's quill,
To grave those lines through which the soul
doth speak,
And pours in timid tones, the hymn at eve.
She from the pictur'd page, doth scan the tribes
That revel in the air, or cleave the flood,
Or roam the wild, delighting much to know
Their various natures, and their habits all,

From the huge elephant, to the smal fly
That liveth but a day, yet in that day
Is happy, and outspreads a shining wing,
Exulting in the mighty Maker's care.
She weeps that men should barb the monarch-whale,
In his wild ocean-home, and wound the dove,
And snare the pigeon, hasting to its nest
To feed its young, and hunt the flying deer,
And find a pleasure in the pain he gives.
She tells the sweetly modulated tale
To her young brother, and devoutly cheers
At early morning, seated on his knee
Her hoary grandsire from the Book of God
Who meekly happy in his fourscore years,
Mourns not the dimness gathering o'er his sight
But with a saintly kindness, bows him down
To drink from her young lip, the lore he loves.
Fond, gentle child, who like a flower that hastes
To burst its sheath, hath come so quickly forth
A sweet companion, walking by my side,—
Thou, whom thy father loveth, and thy friends
Delight to praise, lift thy young heart to God,—
That whatsoe'er doth please him in thy life
He may perfect, and by his Spirit's power
Remove each germ of evil, that thy soul
When this brief discipline of time is o'er
May rise to praise him with an angel's song.

FAREWELL TO THE AGED.

RISE weary spirit, to a realm of rest!
  Sorrow hath had her will of thee, and Pain,
With a destroyer's fury prob'd thy breast,
  But thou the victory through Christ didst gain:
      Rise free from stain.

Years wrote their history on thy furrow'd brow
  In withering lines; and Time like ocean's foam
Swept o'er the shores of hope, till thou didst know
  Earth's emptiness. But now no more to roam
      Pass to thy home.

Blest filial Love reserv'd its freshest wreath
  Of changeless green and blooming buds for thee,
And o'er thy bosom threw its grateful breath,
  When the waste world but weeds of misery
      Spread for thine eye.

Take up the triumph-song, thou who didst bow
So long and meekly 'neath the Chastener's rod,
Thou whose firm faith beheld with raptur'd glow
The resurrection cleave the burial-sod,
Go to thy God.

THY WILL BE DONE.

WHEN with unclouded ray
  Shines the bright sun,
When summer streamlets play,
And all around is gay,
Then shall the spirit say,
  "Thy will be done?"

No.—When the flowers of love
  Fade, one by one,
When in its blasted grove
The shuddering heart doth rove,
Then say, and look above,
  "*Thy will be done.*"

DEATH OF MRS. H. W. L. WINSLOW, MISSIONARY IN CEYLON.

Thy name hath power like magic. Back it brings
The earliest pictures hung in memory's halls,
Tinting them freshly o'er:—the rugged cliff,—
The towering trees,— the wintry walk to school,—
The page so often conn'd,—the hour of sport
Well earn'd and dearly priz'd,—the sparkling brook
Making its slight cascade,—the darker rush
Of the pent river through its rocky pass,—
The violet-gatherings 'mid the vernal banks,—
When our young hearts did ope their crystal gates
To every simple joy.
I little deem'd,
'Mid all that gay and gentle fellowship,
That Asia's sun would beam upon thy grave,
Tho', even then, from thy dark, serious eye
There was a glancing forth of glorious thought,

That scorn'd earth's vanities. I saw thee stand
With but a few brief summers o'er thy head,
And in the consecrated courts of God
Confess thy Saviour's name. And they who mark'd
The promise of that opening bud did ask
What its full bloom must be.
But now thy couch
Is where the Ceylon mother tells her child
Of all thy prayers and labours. Yes, thy rest
Is in the bosom of that fragrant isle
Where heathen man, with lavish Nature strives
To blot the lesson she would teach of God

Thy pensive sisters pause upon thy tomb
To catch the spirit that did bear thee through
All tribulation, till thy robes were white,
To join the angelic train. And so farewell,
My childhood's playmate, aud my sainted friend,
Whose bright example, not without rebuke,
Admonisheth, that home, and ease, and wealth,
And native l nd, are well exchang'd for heaven.

"I WILL ARISE AND GO UNTO MY FATHER."

WANDERER, amid the snares
Of Time's uncertain way,
Of thousand nameless fears the sport,
Of countless ills the prey :

A stranger 'mid the land
Where thy probation lies,
In peril from each adverse blast
And e'en from prosperous skies.

In peril from thy friends,
In peril from thy foes,
In peril from the rebel heart
That in thy bosom glows;

Hast thou no Father's house
Beyond this pilgrim scene,
That thou on Earth's delusive props
With bleeding breast doth lean?

Yet not a Mother's care
  Who for her infant sighs,
When absence shuts it from her arms
  Or sickness dims its eyes,

Transcends the love divine,
  The welcome full and free
With which the glorious King of Heaven
  Will stretch his arms to thee,

When thou with contrite tear
  Shall wait within his walls,
Imploring but the broken bread
  That from his table falls.

No more his mansion shun,
  No more distrust his grace,
Turn from the orphanage of earth
  And find a Sire's embrace.

VOICE FROM THE GRAVE OF A SUNDAY SCHOOL TEACHER.

YES this is the holy ground,
Lay me to slumber here,
The cherish'd thoughts of early days,
Have made this spot most dear,—
Fast by the hallow'd church
Where first I learned to pray
In faith, and penitence and peace,—
Make ye my bed of clay.

Though life hath been to me
A scene of joy and love,
And sweet affections round my heart
Unchanging garlands wove,
Though knowledge in its power
At studious midnight came,
Enkindling in my raptur'd mind,
A bright, unwavering flame;

Yet dearer far than all,
Was Heaven's celestial lore·

Then come, belov'd and youthful train,
  Who hear my voice no more
Come, sing the hymn I taught,
  Here, by my lowly bed,
And with your Sabbath-lessons blend
  Sweet memories of the dead.

—

ON THE DEATH OF A MEMBER OF THE INFANT SCHOOL.

"He gathereth the lambs with his arm, and carrieth them in his bosom."—ISAIAH.

LAMB! in a clime of verdure,
  Thy favored lot was cast,
No serpent 'mid thy flow'ry food,
  Upon thy fold no blast,—
Thine were the crystal fountains,
  And thine a cloudless sky,
Amid thy sports a star of love
  Thy playmate brother's eye.

Approving guides caress'd thee,
  Where'er thy footsteps rov'd,
The ear that heard thee bless'd thee,
  The eye that saw thee lov'd;
Yet life hath snares and sorrows
  From which no friend can save,

And evils might have thronged thy path,
  Which thou wert weak to brave.

There is a heavenly Shepherd,
  And ere thy infant charms
Had caught the tinge of care or woe
  He call'd thee to his arms,
And though the shadowy valley,
  With Death's dark frown was dim,
Light cheer'd the stormy passage
  And thou art safe with *Him*.

DEATH OF A YOUNG MUSICIAN.

Music was in thy heart, and fast entwin'd,
And closely knotted with its infant strings,
Were the rich chords of melody. When youth
And science led thee to their classic bower,
A pale and patient student, the lone lamp
Of midnight vigil found thee pouring out
Thy soul in dulcet sound. In memory's cell
Still live those thrilling tones, as erst they broke,
Beguiling with sweet choral symphonies
The festal hour.
But, lo! while thou didst wake
The solemn organ to entrancing power,
Tracing the secret spells of harmony,
On through deep rapture's labyrinthine maze
Devotion came, and breath'd upon thy brow,
And made her temple in thy tuneful breast.
So, music led thee to thy Saviour's feet,
Serene and true disciple, and their harps
Who fondly hold untiring guardianship
O'er frail man's pilgrim path, were tremulous
With joy for thee.

Nor vainly to thy soul
Came Heaven's high message wrapp'd in minstrelsy,
For to its service, with unshrinking zeal,
The blossom of thy life was dedicate.
Thy hand was on God's altar, when a touch,
Sudden and strange and icy cold, unloos'd
Its fervent grasp. Thy gentle heart was glad
With the soft promise of a hallow'd love.
But stern death dash'd it out. Now there are tears
In tenderest eyes for thee.
Yet we who know
That earth hath many discords for a soul
Fine-ton'd and seraph-strung, and that the feet
Which fain would follow Christ are sometimes held
In the dark meshes of a downward course,
Till strong repentance urge them back with tears,
Do feel thy gain.
'Tis well thou art at home,
Spirit of melody and peace and love.

THE SOUTH-AMERICAN STATUES.

There are still found, upon the snow-covered cliffs of the Andes, the bodies of some of those Spaniards, who after the discovery of America, in searching for the rich mines, that had been described to them in Peru, took a circuitous route among the mountains, and perished by the cold, which petrified them into statues.

Why seek ye out such dizzy height
  Amid yon drear domain?
Why choose ye cells with frost-work white
  Ye haughty men of Spain?
The Condor, on his mighty wing
  Doth scale your cloud-wreathed walls,
But to his scream their caverns ring,
  As from the cliff he falls.

The poor Peruvian scans with dread
  Your fix'd and stony eye,
The timid child averts his head,
  And faster hurries by

They from the fathers of the land
  Have heard your withering tale,
Nor spare to mock the tyrant band
  Transformed to statues pale.

Ye came to grasp the Indian's gold,
  Ye scorn'd his feathery dart,
But Andes rose, that monarch old,
  And took his children's part,
And with that strange embalming art
  Which ancient Egypt knew,
He threw his frost-chain o'er your heart,
  As to his breast ye grew.

He chain'd you while strong manhood's tide
  Did through your bosoms roll
Upon your lip the curl of pride,
  And avarice in your soul.
Strange slumber stole with mortal pang
  Across the frozen plain,
And thunderblasts your sentence rang,
  "Sleep and ne'er wake again."

Uprose the moon, the Queen of night
  Danc'd with the Protean tide,
And years fulfill'd their measur'd flight,
  And ripening ages died,
Slow centuries in oblivion's flood
  Sank like the tossing wave.

But changeless and transfix'd ye stood,
  The dead without a grave.

The infant wrought its flowery span
  On Love's maternal breast,
And whiten'd to a hoary man,
  And laid him down to rest,
Race after race, with weary moan
  Went to their dreamless sleep,
While ye, upon your feet of stone,
  Perpetual penance keep.

How little deem'd ye, when ye hurl'd
  Your challenge o'er the main,
And vow'd to teach a new-born world
  The vassalage of Spain,
Thus till the doom's-day cry of pain
  Shall rive your prison-rock,
To bear upon your brow like Cain,
  A mark that all might mock.

But long from high Castilian bowers
  Look'd forth the inmates fair,
And gave the tardy midnight hours
  To watching and despair,
Oft starting as some light guitar
  Its breath of sweetness shed,
Yet lord and lover linger'd far
  Till life's brief vision fled.

Their vaunted tournament is o'er,
  Their knightly lance in rest,
Ambition's fever burns no more
  Within their conquering breast,
For high between the earth and skies
  Check'd in their venturous path,
A fearful monument they rise,
  Of Andes' vengeful wrath.

AGRICULTURE.

The hero hath his fame,
  'Tis blazon'd on his tomb;
But earth withholds her glad acclaim,
  And frowns in silent gloom:
His footsteps on her breast
  Were like the Simoom's blast,
And Death's dark ravages attest
  Where'er the Conqueror past.

By him her harvests sank,
  Her famish'd flocks were slain,
And from the fount where thousands drank
  Came gushing blood like rain;
For him no requiem-sigh
  From vale or grove shall swell,
But flowers exulting lift their eye,
  Where the proud spoiler fell.

Look at yon peaceful bands
  Who guide the glittering share,
The quiet labour of whose hands
  Doth make Earth's bosom fair

For them the rich perfume
  From ripen'd fields doth flow,
They bid the desert rose to bloom,
  The wild with plenty glow.

Ah! happier thus to prize
  The humble, rural shade,
And like our Father in the skies
  Blest Nature's work to aid,
Than famine and despair
  Among mankind to spread,
And Earth our mother's curse to bear
  Down to the silent dead.

FUNERAL OF A PHYSICIAN.

There was a throng within the temple-gates,
And more of sorrow on each thoughtful brow
Than seemed to fit the sacred day of praise.
Neighbour on neighbour gaz'd, and friend on friend,
Yet few saluted; for the sense of loss
Weigh'd heavy in each bosom. Aged men
Bowed down their reverend heads in wondering woe,
That he who so retain'd the ardent smile
And step elastic of life's morning prime,
Should fall before them. Stricken at his side
Were friendships of no common fervency
Or brief endurance; for his cheering tone
And the warm pressure of his hand, restor'd
Young recollections, scenes of boyhood's bliss,
And the unwounded trust of guileless years.
—The men of skill, who cope with stern disease,
And wear Hygeia's mantle, offering still
Fresh incense at her shrine, with sighs deplore
A brother and a guide. But can ye tell
How many now amid this gather'd throng

In tender meditations deeply muse,
Coupling his image with their gratitude?
He had stood with them at the gate of death,
And pluck' them from the spoiler's threatening grasp,
Or, when the roses from their pilgrimage
Were shorn, walk'd humbly with them 'neath the cloud
Of God's displeasure. Such remembrances
Rush o'er their spirits with a whelming tide,
Till in the heart's deep casket tribute tears
Lie thick, like pearls. And doubt not there are those
'Mid this assembly, in the scanty robes
Of penury half wrapt, who well might tell
Of ministrations at their couch of woe,
Of toil-spent nights, and timely charities,
Uncounted, save in heaven.
'Tis well!—'Tis well!
The parted benefactor justly claims
Such obsequies. Yet let the Gospel breathe
Its strain sublime. A hallow'd hand hath cull'd
From the deep melodies of David's lyre,
And from the burning eloquence of Paul,
Balm from the mourner's wound. But there's a group
Within whose sacred home yon lifeless form
Had been the centre of each tender hope,
The soul of every joy. Affections pure
And patriarchal hospitality,

Like household deities, presiding, spread
Their wings around, making the favour'd cell
As bright a transcript of lost Eden's bliss,
As beams below. Now round that shaded hearth
The polish'd brow of radiant beauty droops,
Like the pale lily-flower, by pitiless storms
Press'd and surcharg'd. There too are sadden'd eyes
More eloquent than words, and bursting hearts;
Earth may not heal such grief. '*Tis heal'd in heaven.*

NATURE'S BEAUTY.

I looked on nature's beauty, and it came
Like a blest spirit to my inmost heart,
And sadness fled away. The fragrant breeze
Swept o'er me, as a tale of other times,
Lifting the curtain from the ancient cells
Of early memory. The young vine put forth
Her quivering tendrils, while the patron bough
Lured their light clasping, with such love as leaves
Do whisper to each other, when they lean
To drink the music of the summer-shower.

There was a sound of wings, and through the mesh,
Of her green latticed chamber, stole the bird
To cheer her callow young. The stream flowed on,
And on its lake-like breast, the bending trees
Did glass themselves with such serene repose
That their still haunt seemed holy. The spent sun

Turned to his rest, and soft his parting ray
To mountain-top, and spire, and verdant grove,
And burnished casement, and reposing nest.
Spake benediction. And the vesper-strain
Went breathing up from every plant and flower.

The rose did fold itself, as though it caught
From some high minaret, the cry, "To prayer!"
At which the Moslem kneels; and the blue eye
Of the young violet, look'd devoutly forth
As looks the shepherd, from his cottage door
When the clear horn doth warn the Alpine cliffs
To praise the Lord. And then the queenly moon
Came through heaven's portal. High her vestal train
Did bear their brilliant cressets in their hands—
Trembling with pride and pleasure. Beauty lay
Like a broad mantle on each slumbering dell
And to the domes, that peered through woven shades
Gave Attic grace.
'Twere sweet to bear away
And keep the precious picture in my heart
Of these sweet woods, and waters, summer-drest
And angel-voic'd—until I lay me down
On the low pillow of my last repose.

SENTIMENT IN A SERMON.

"Piety flourishes best, in a soil watered by tears, and often succeeds, where harvests of temporal good have failed."

HOPE'S soft petals love the beam
 That cheer'd them into birth;—
Pleasure seeks a glittering stream
 Bright oozing from the earth;—
Knowledge yields his lofty fruit
 To those who climb with toil,
But Heaven's pure plant strikes deepest root
 Where tears have dew'd the soil.

Hope with flow'rets strews the blast
 When adverse winds arise;
Pleasure's garlands wither fast
 Before inclement skies;
Knowledge often mocks pursuit,
 Involv'd in mazy shade,
But Piety yields richer fruit
 When earthly harvests fade.

THE POWER OF FRIENDSHIP.

AN ANCIENT LEGEND OF FRANCONIA.

'Twas midnight on the Gaulish plains,
And foes were mustering near;
For there Franconia's warriors frown'd,
With battle-axe and spear.

Untented on the earth they lay
Beneath a summer sky,
While on their slumbering host, the Moon
Look'd down with wistful eye,

As if reproachfully she sigh'd
"Oh ye of transient breath!
How can ye rise from rest so sweet
To do the deeds of death!"

Discoursing mid the sleeping train
Two noble youths were found;
Their graceful limbs recumbent thrown
Upon the dewy ground.

Bold Carloman's undaunted mien
  A hero's spirit show'd,
Though Beauty on his lip and brow
  Had made her soft abode.

And Merovee's dark, hazle eye
  Like flashing fire was bright,
As thus with flowing words he charm'd
  The leaden ear of night.

"Methinks 'twere sweet once more to see
  Our native, forest shade,
And the wild streamlet leaping free
  Along the sparkling glade,

"With merry shout, at peep of dawn,
  The hunter's toil to join,
Or in the tiny boat launch forth
  And rule the billowy Rhine."

He paused,—but Carloman replied,
  "Lurks not some spell behind?—
Why doth thy courtier-tongue delay
  To name fair Rosalind?

'Those raven locks, that lofty brow,
  That ebon eye of pride,
With firm, yet tender glance, might well
  Beseem a warrior's bride."

With trembling voice he scarce pursued,
  "Why should we shrink, to say
How much we both have loved the maid?
  Yet on our parting day—

"Her farewell words to me were kind,
  They flow'd in silver tone,
But ah! the tear-drop of the soul
  Was shed for thee alone.

"If in to-morrow's bloody fray,
  I slumber with the slain,
And thou survive, with joy to greet
  Our native vales again,

"O bear to her so long adored
  My dying wish,"—in vain
To weave the tissued thoughts he strove,
  For tears fell down like rain.

Thrice Merovee the mourner's hand
  Wrung hard, and would have said,
"Fear not that Love's insidious shaft
  Shall strike our friendship dead!"

He thrice essay'd,—yet still was mute;—
  Then loosed his bossy shield,
And laid him down as if to sleep
  Upon the verdant field.

He laid him down, but wakeful woe
  His weary heart amazed,
And by the pale moon's waning ray
  On Carloman he gazed.

The pastimes of their boyish years,
  The confidence of youth,
And holy Friendship's treasur'd vow
  Of everlasting truth,

Came thronging o'er his generous soul,
  And ere the dawn of day,
Up from his restless couch he rose,
  And wander'd lone away.

But Carloman in broken sleep
  Still roved with troubled mind,
Oft in his dark dream murmuring deep,
  "Adieu, my Rosalind!"

Then in his ear a thrilling voice
  Exclaim'd "Brave youth,—arise!
The morn that lights to glorious strife
  With purple flouts the skies:—

No lover to his bridal hastes
  With spirit half so warm,
As rush Franconia's sons to meet
  Red battle's moody storm."

Abash'd the youthful sleeper sprang,
And Merovee stood near,
An iron chain was in his hand,
And on his brow a tear.

Then quickly round the forms of both
That stubborn band he threw,
And joined the parted links in one,
And set the rivet true.

"Think'st thou I'd cross the rolling Rhine
And see our forests wave,
And urge my suit to Rosalind
When thou wert in thy grave?

"No!—by yon golden orb that rolls
In splendor through the air,
If honour's death this day be thine,
That holy death I'll share."

They arm'd them for the battle-field,
Their blood was boiling high,
Forgot were danger, love, and woe,
In that proud ecstacy;

Forgot was she, whose hand alone
Could give their hope its meed,
Forgot was all in earth or heaven
Save their dear country's need.

Their rushing legions like the surge
  When tempests lash the main,
With thundering shout and revelry
  Spread o'er the fatal plain.

Forth came the cavalry of Gaul,
  With glittering lance and spur,
Led on by warlike Constantine,
  That Christian Emperor.

With cloud of darts and clash of swords
  They greet the early sun,
And when his western gate he sought
  The conflict scarce was done.

But sober twilight's mantle grey
  Enwrapt a silent plain,
Save where from wounded bosoms burst
  The lingering groan of pain.

Crush'd forms were there, where stubborn life
  Still for the mastery pined,
Stern brows, where death had pass'd, and left
  The frown of hate behind.

And mid that ghastly train were seen
  Two victims young and fair,
The chain that bound their polish'd breasts
  Reveal'd what youths they were.

Bold toward the sky, the marble brow
  Of Carloman was turn'd,
And firm his right hand grasp'd the sword
  As if some foe he spurn'd;

His ample shield was fondly flung,
  To guard his partner's breast,
And Merovee's pale, bloomless lips
  Upon his cheek were prest;—

While weltering in the purple stream
  That dyed their garments' fold,
Their flowing curls profusely lay,
  Bright chesnut blent with gold.

And eyes that wept such fate, might read
  Upon their bosom's chain,
That *once* when Love and Friendship strove
  The power of Love was vain.

THE GARDEN.

"*Gardens* have been the scenes of the three most stupendous events that have occurred on earth:—the temptation and fall of man—the agony of the Son of God—and his resurrection from the grave."—NOTES *of the American Editor of* KEBLE'S CHRISTIAN YEAR."

Is't not a holy place, thy garden's bound,
Peopled with plants, and every living leaf
Instinct with thought, to stir the musing mind?
—Where was it that our Mother wandering went,
When 'mid her nursling vines and flowers, she met
The gliding serpent in his green and gold,
And rashly listen'd to his glozing tongue,
Till loss of Eden and the wrath of God
Did fade from her remembrance? Was it not
A garden, where this deed of rashness check'd
The stainless blossom of a world unborn?
—Still, tread with trembling. Hast *thou* nought to fear?

No tempter in *thy* path, with power to sow
Thy Paradise with thorns, if God permit?
So, hold thy way amid the sweets of earth
With cautious step, and have thy trust above?
—Is't not a holy place, thy garden's bound,
When at the cool close of the summer's day
Thou lingerest there, indulging sweet discourse
With lips belov'd? Then speak of Him who bare
Upon his tortur'd brow, strange dews of blood
For man's redemption.
Bring the thrilling scene
Home to thine inmost soul:—the sufferer's cry,
"Father! if it be possible, this cup
Take thou away.—*Yet not my will but thine*:"
The sleeping friends who could not watch one hour,
The torch, the flashing sword, the traitor's kiss,
The astonish'd angel with the tear of Heaven
Upon his cheek, still striving to assuage
Those fearful pangs that bow'd the Son of God
Like a bruis'd reed. Thou who hast power to look
Thus at Gethsemane, *be still! be still!*
What are thine insect-woes compared to his
Who agonizeth there? Count thy brief pains
As the dust-atom on life's chariot wheels,
And in a Saviour's grief forget them all.
—Is't not a holy place, thy garden's bound?
"Look to the sepulchre!" said they of Rome.

"And set a seal upon it." So, the guard
Who knew that sleep was death, stood with fix'd
eye
Watching the garden-tomb, which proudly hid
The body of the crucified.
Whose steps
'Mid the ill stifled sob of woman's grief
Prevent the dawn? Yet have they come too
late,
For *He* is risen,—*He* hath burst the tomb,
Whom 'twas not possible for Death to hold.
Yea, his pierced hand did cleave the heavens, to
share
That resurrection, which the "slow of heart"
Shrank to believe.
Fain would I, on this spot,
So holy, ponder, till the skies grow dark,
And sombre evening spreads her deepest pall.
—Come to my heart, thou Wisdom that dost
grow
In the chill coffin of the shrouded dead,
Come to my heart. For silver hairs may spring
Thick o'er the temples, yet the soul fall short
Even of that simple rudiment which dwells
With babes in Christ. I would be taught of
thee,
Severe Instructor, who dost make thy page
Of pulseless breasts and unimpassion'd brows,
And lips that yield no sound. Thou who dost
wake

Man for that lesson which he reads ou. once,
And mak'st thy record of the sullen mounds
That mar the church-yard's smoothness, let me
glean
Wisdom among the tombs, for I would learn
Thy deep, unflattering lore. What have I said?
No! not of thee, but of the hand that pluck'd
The sceptre from thee.
Thou, who once didst taste
Of all man's sorrows, save the guilt of sin,—
Divine Redeemer! teach us so to walk
In these our earthly gardens, as to gain
Footing at last, amid the trees of God,
Which by the Eternal River from His Throne
Nourish'd, shall never fade.

VICE.

In vain the heart that goes astray
From virtue's seraph-guarded way,—
May hope that feelings, just and free,
Meek peace,—or firm integrity,—
Or innocence, with snowy vest
Will condescend to be its guest.
——As soon within the viper's cell
Might pure and white-wing'd spirits dwell,
As soon the flame of vivid gleam
Glow in the chill and turbid stream;—
For by strong links, a viewless chain
Connects our wanderings with our pain,—
And Heaven ordains it thus, to show,
That bands of vice, are bonds of woe.

THE SWEDISH LOVERS.

Where Dalecarlia's pine-clad hills
  Rear high in air the untrodden snow,
Where her scant vales and murmuring rills
  A short and sultry summer know,

Where great Gustavus exiled, fled,
  And found beneath a covering rude
Hearts by the noblest impulse led
  Of valour, faith, and fortitude,

There still, a virtuous race retain
  The simple manners of their sires,
Unchanged by love of sordid gain,
  Or stern ambition's restless fires,

And there, where silver Mora flow'd,
  In freshness through the changeful wild,
A peasant rear'd his lone abode,
  And fair Ulrica was his child.

Untutor'd by the arts that spoil
  The soul's integrity was she,
And nurtur'd in the virtuous toil
  Of unpretending poverty.

Within a neighbouring hamlet's bound,
  In manly beauty's ardent grace,
Christiern his humble dwelling found
  Amid the miner's hardy race.

He oft beheld Ulrica's hand
  A part in rural labour take,
To bind the sheaf with pliant band,
  Or steer the light boat o'er the lake.

He mark'd the varying toil bestow
  On her pure cheek a richer dye,
And saw enlivening spirits flow
  In dazzing radiance from her eye.

Oft in the holy house of prayer
  Where weekly crowds assembling bow
He mark'd the meek and reverent air
  Which shed new lustre o'er her brow.

And soon no joy his heart might share
  Unless her soft smile met his view,
And soon he thought no scene was fair
  Unless her eye admired it too.

And duly as the shadows fleet
  O'er closing day, with silence fraught,
Young Christiern with his lute so sweet
  Ulrica's peaceful mansion sought.

Long had the gossip's mystic speech
  Deep knowledge of their love profest,
Before the timid lip of each
  The cherish'd secret had exprest.

But when the trembling pain reveal'd,
  And vows of mutual faith had cheer'd,
Quick on the hamlet's verdant field
  Christiern their simple cottage rear'd.

And taught Ulrica's rose to twine
  Its tendrils round the rustic door,
And thought how sweet at day's decline
  When the accustom'd task was o'er,

To sit and pour the evening song
  Amid gay summer's varied bloom,
And catch the breeze that bore along
  Her favourite flowret's rich perfume.

The appointed day its course begun
  With gentle beams of rosy light,
When they whose hearts had long been one
  Should join their hands in hallow'd rite.

At morn the marriage bell was rung,
  Where the lone spire from chapel towers,
And village maids assembling hung
  Ulrica's lowly hall with flowers.

Yet mark'd a shade that pensively
  Was stealing o'er her features fair,
For mid those hours of festive glee
  The youthful bridegroom came not there.

Full oft along the coppice green
  She deem'd his well-known step she heard,
Then brightening, rais'd her lovely mein,
  Then sigh'd—for other guest appear'd.

Dim twilight o'er the landscape fell,
  Sad evening paced its tardy round,
Nor Christiern at his father's cell,
  Nor through the hamlet's range was found.

"'Tis but in sport,"—her neighbours cried,
  "The temper of your heart to prove."—
"Not thus," the sinking maid replied,
  "Doth *Christiern* sport with trusting love."

Night came, but void of rest or sleep
  Move on its watches dark and slow,
Ulrica laid her down to weep
  In anguish of unutter'd woe.

How drear the gentle dawn appear'd!
  How gloomy morning's rosy ray!
Nor tidings of her lover cheer'd
  The horrors of that lengthen'd day.

Weeks past away,—all search was vain—
Her smile of lingering hope was dead,
She shunned the joyous village train,
And from each rural pastime fled.

Time wrote his history on her brow!
In characters of woe severe,
And furrows mark'd the ceaseless flow
Of fearful sorrow's burning tear.

Years roll'd on years,—her friends decay'd,
Her seventieth winter chill had flown,
A new and alter'd race survey'd
The spectre stranger sad and lone.

"Why do I live?"—she sometimes sigh'd,
"Thus crush'd beneath affliction's rod?"—
But stern reproving thought replied,
"Ask not such question of thy God!"

Yet still she lov'd that pine-clad hill
Where erst her love his way would take,
Still wander'd near his favourite rill
Or sat by Mora's glassy lake.

His white-wash'd cot with roses gay,
Had lone and tenantless been kept,
But moulder'd now in time's decay,
And mid its ruins oft she wept.

The sound of flail at early morn,
Or harvest song of happy hind,
Awoke undying memory's thorn
To probe anew her wounded mind.

Where near her cell, the quarries bold
With veins metallic richly glow,
And where their yawning chasms unfold
Dark entrance to the depths below.

Once, while the miners toil'd to trace,
Between two shafts an opening new,
Mid earth and stones, *a human face*
Glared sudden on their startled view.

A form erect, of manly size,
In that embalming niche reposed,
And slight and carelessly the eyes
As if in recent dreams were closed.

The sunburnt tinge that bronzed the brow
Was bleach'd within that humid shade,
And o'er the smooth-cheek's florid glow
The raven curls profusely play'd.

The pliant hand was soft and fair,
As if in youth's unfolding prime,
Altho' the bridal robes declare
The costume of an ancient time.

Yet no recorded fact might tell
  Who fill'd that dark mysterious shrine,
The hoariest ones remember'd well
  A shock which whelm'd that ruin'd mine

But all of him who lifeless slept,
  Was lost in time's unfathom'd deep;
At length an aged woman crept
  To join the throng who gaze and weep.

Propp'd on her staff she totter'd near,
  But when the cold corse met her eye,
She clasp'd her hands in pangs severe,
  And shrieks revealed her agony.

And fainting on the earth she lay,
  With struggles of convulsive breath,
As if weak life had fled away
  In terror at the sight of death.

Yet when their care again could light
  The vital taper's fading flame,
When day assured her doubtful sight,
  Deep sighs and sobs of anguish came.

No word of notice or reply
  She deign'd to their inquiring tone,
One only object fix'd her eye,
  One image fill'd her heart alone.

'Twas thus, disdaining all relief,
She mourn'd with agonizing strife,
While the wild storm of love and grief
Rack'd the worn ligaments of life.

'Twas thus o'er age and sorrow's gloom,
Unchill'd affection soar'd sublime,
While strangely foster'd in the tomb
Youth rose, to mock the power of time.

That shrivell'd form convulsed so long,
And that bright brow devoid of breath,
Gleam'd forth in contradiction strong,
Like buried life, and living death.

'Twas strange from livid lips to hear
Such wild lament, such piercing groan,
While manly love reposing near,
Call'd forth, yet heeded not the moan.

The mourner raised the curls whose shade
Conceal'd that polish'd forehead dear,
And there her wasted hand she laid,
Exclaiming in the lifeless ear,

"Oh!—have I lived to see that face
Engraved upon my soul so deep?
And in this bitterness to trace,
Those features wrapt in holy sleep?

My promised love!—thou still hast kept
  The beauty of thy mantling prime,
While o'er my broken frame have crept
  The wrinkles and the scars of time.

Yes.—Well may I be wreck'd and torn
  Whom fifty adverse years have seen
Like blasted oak, the whirlwind's scorn
  Still clinging where my joys *had been.*

My boughs and blossoms all were reft,—
  They might not know a second birth,—
Why were my wither'd roots thus left
  Unhappy cumberers of the earth?

Yet still one image soothed my cares,
  Amid my nightly dream would shine,
Came hovering fondly o'er my prayers
  And this, my buried lord, was thine.

That smile!—ah, still unchanged it plays
  O'er thy pure cheek's vermilion hue,
As when it met my childhood's gaze,
  Or charm'd my youth's delighted view,—

As when thy skilful hand would bring
  From mountain's breast, or shelter'd down,
The earliest buds of tardy spring
  To scatter o'er my tresses brown.

But now the blossoms of the tomb
Have whiten'd all those ringlets gay,
Whilst thou in bright perennial bloom,
Dost shine superior to decay.

Rend from thy lip that marble seal,
And bid once more those accents flow,
That waked even coldest hearts to feel,
And taught forgetfulness to woe.

Wildly I rave!—as if thine ears
The sad recital would receive;
Vainly I weep!—as if those tears
Could move thy sainted soul to grieve.

Time was, when Christiern's treasur'd name
No voice howe'er despised might speak,
But from my bounding heart there came
A tide of crimson o'er the cheek;

Time was, when Christiern's step was heard
With raptur'd joy's tumultuous swell,
And wher his least and lightest word,
Was stored in memory's choicest cell.

Yet have I lived to mourn thee lost,
To find each earthly solace fled,
And now, on time's last billow tost,
To see thee rising from the dead!

Ha!—didst thou speak,--and call my soul
  To bowers where roses ever bloom,
Where boundless tides of pleasure roll,
  And deathless love defies the tomb?

I come! I come!"—Strange lustre fired
  Her glazing eye, and all was o'er,
No more that heaving breast respired,
  And earthly sorrows pain'd no more.

So there they lay, a lifeless pair,
  Those hearts by youthful love entwined
Sever'd by fate, and fix'd despair,
  Were now in death's cold union join'd.

Full oft in Dalecarlian cells
  When evening shadows darkly droop,
Some hoary-headed peasant tells
  Their story to a listening group.

And oft the wondering child willl weep
  The pensive youth unconscious sigh,
At hapless Christiern's fearful sleep,
  And sad Ulrica's constancy.

TO THE MOON.

HAIL, beauteous and inconstant!— Thou who roll'st
Thy silver car around the realm of night,
Queen of soft hours! how fanciful art thou
In equipage and vesture.—Now thou com'st
With slender horn piercing the western cloud,
As erst on Judah's hills, when joyous throngs
With trump and festival, saluted thee;
Anon thy waxing crescent 'mid the host
Of constellations, like some fairy boat,
Glides o'er the waveless sea; then as a bride
Thou bow'st thy cheek behind a fleecy veil,
Timid and fair; or, bright in regal robes,
Dost bid thy full-orb'd chariot roll,
Sweeping with silent rein the starry path
Up to the highest node,—then plunging low,
To seek dim Nadir in his misty cell.
—Lov'st thou our Earth, that thou dost hold thy lamp
To guide and cheer her, when the wearied Sun
Forsakes her?—Sometimes, roving on, thou shedd'st

The eclipsing plot ungrateful, on thy sire
Who feeds thy urn with light,—but sinking deep
'Neath the dark shadow of the earth dost mourn
And find thy retribution.
--Dost thou hold
Dalliance with Ocean, that his mighty heart
Tosses at thine approach, and his mad tides,
Drinking thy favouring glance, more rudely lash
Their rocky bulwark?—Do thy children trace
Through crystal tube our coarser-featured orb
Even as we gaze on thee? With Euclid's art
Perchance, from pole to pole, her sphere they
span,
Her sun-loved tropics—and her spreading seas
Rich with their myriad isles. Perchance they
mark
Where India's cliffs the trembling cloud invade,
Or Andes with his fiery banner floats
The empyrean,—where old Atlas towers,—
Or that rough chain whence he of Carthage
pour'd
Terrors on Rome.—Thou, too, perchance, hast
nursed
Some bold Copernicus, or fondly call'd
A Galileo forth, those sun-like souls
Which shone in darkness, though our darkness
fail'd
To comprehend them.—Cans't thou boast, like
earth,
A Kepler, skilful pioneer and wise?—

A sage to write his name among the stars
Like glorious Herschel?—or a dynasty,
Like great Cassini's, which from sire to son
Transmitted science as a birthright seal'd?
—Rose there some lunar Horrox,—to whose glance
Resplendent Venus her adventurous course
Reveal'd, even in his boyhood?—some La Place
Luminous as the skies he sought to read?—
Thou deign'st no answer,—or I fain would ask
If since thy bright creation, thou hast seen
Aught like a Newton, whose admitted eye
The arcana of the Universe explored?
Light's subtle ray its mechanism disclosed,
The impetuous comet his mysterious lore
Unfolded,—system after system rose,
Eternal wheeling thro' the immensity of space
And taught him of their laws. Even angels stood
Amaz'd as when in ancient times they saw
On Sinai's top, a mortal walk with God.
—But he, to whom the secrets of the skies
Were whisper'd,—in humility adored,
Breathing with childlike reverence the prayer
—"When on yon heavens, with all their orbs I gaze,
Jehovah! what is man?"

TO THE EVENING PRIMROSE.

Pale Primrose! lingering for the evening star
To bless thee with its beam,—like some fair child
Who, ere he rests on Morpheus' downy car
Doth wait his mother's blessing, pure and mild
To hallow his gay dream. His red lips breathe
The prompted prayer, fast by that parent's knee,
Even as thou rear'st thy sweetly fragrant wreath
To matron Evening, while she smiles on thee.

Go to thy rest, pale flower! the star hath shed
His benison, upon thy bosom fair,
The dews of summer bathe thy pensive head
And weary man forgets his daily care;—
Sleep on, my rose! till morning gilds the sky
And bright Aurora's kiss, unseals thy trembling eye.

IMITATION OF PARTS OF THE

PROPHET AMOS.

I, FROM no princely stock, or lineage came,
Nor bore my sire, a prophet's honour'd name,—
But 'mid the Tekoan shepherds' manners rude,
My speech was fashion'd, and my toil pursued.

O'er hills and dales I led,—o'er streams and rocks,
The wandering footsteps of my herds, and flocks,—
I fed them where the fruitful vallies fling
Their first, fresh verdure, on the lap of spring;
Or where the quiet fountains slowly glide
Their fringed eyes, among the flowers to hide;—
And when the noontide sun, with fervid heat
Upon the tender lambs, too fiercely beat,
I guided, where the mountain's sheltering head,
A sable shade, across the landscape spread.
There, while they sank in slumber, soft and meek,
I wandered forth, my simple meal to seek,

The juicy wild fig, and the crystal tide
My strength renew'd, and nature's wants supplied.

When sober twilight drew her curtaining shade,
And on the dewy lawn my flocks were laid,—
In my rough mantle, by their side reclined
I gave to holy thoughts my wakeful mind;—
The stars, that in their mystic circles move,
The sparkling blue, of the high arch above,—
The pomp of eve, the storm's majestic power,
The solemn silence of the midnight hour,
The silver softness of the unveil'd moon,
Spake to my soul of Him, the Everlasting One.

Once as I woke, from visions, high and sweet,
And found my flocks reposing at my feet,
—Saw morning's earliest ray, the hills invest,
Stream o'er the forest, touch the mountain's breast,
Glance o'er the glittering streams and dart its way,
Thro' the damp vales, where slumbering vapours lay,—
Methought, within my heart, a light there shone
More clear, and glorious than the rising sun,—
And while my every nerve with rapture thrilled,
A Power Supreme, my soul in silence held.

Quick to the earth, my bending knee I bowed,
My raised eyes fixing on a crimson cloud,—
Which from its cleaving arch, the mandate bore,
"Go shepherd, lead thy much-lov'd flock no more!"—
My trembling lips now press'd the soil I trod,—
"Shepherd, forsake thy flock, and be the seer of God."
Uprising at the heavenly call, I laid
My crook and scrip beneath the spreading shade,
"I go, I go, my God!" my answering spirit said.

Thro' the rude stream I dash'd, whose foaming tide,
Came whitening o'er the mountain's hoary side;
But pressing on my path, I heard with pain,
The approaching footsteps of my cherished train,—
And wept, as gazing on their fleecy pride,
I thought, who now their wandering steps should guide.

Yet still, within, the hallow'd impulse burn'd,
And soon, its answering thoughts my heart return'd;—
"My tender lambs, my unfed flock, adieu,
My God, a shepherd will provide for you,
One kind as I have been, whose care shall guide
You, where fresh pastures smile, and fountains glide;

A hand unseen, a voice and purpose true,
Divide you from my charge, and me from you."

What tho' my rustic speech and shepherd's dress
But ill a prophet's dignity express,—
What tho' the doom I bear, be dark with fear,
And grate repulsive on the guilty ear,—
What tho' my heart beneath fierce tortures break,
And I, a martyr's fiery death partake,—
Yet He, who summoned from yon distant rock,
The rough-clad man to leave his simple flock,
With strength will gird him, for his wants provide,
And quell the clamours of the sons of pride.

With fearless brow, I sought his haughty foes,
Where proud Samaria's regal ramparts rose.
But lo! the wasted suburbs, parch'd and dry
Spread a brown heath, to meet the wondering eye,
The smitten verdure, and the sterile plain,
Disclosed the march of a devouring train,
Before whose face, the fruitful earth was fair
Behind, a prey to famine, bleak and bare.—
The wasted herds, a poor, neglected train,
Sought their accustom'd food, but sought in vain,—

Some, mad with hunger, spurn'd the flinty clay
And some in pangs of death, despairing lay.

Then, low to earth I bent my drooping head,
As one who mourns his dearest idol dead,—
"My God!" I cried, "my God, arise and see,
Thy chosen people's fearful misery!—
The sick land mourns its harden'd children's sin,
Thy wrath devours without and guilt within:—
Ah! who shall drooping Israel's strength repair,
If thou dost cast him from thy succouring care?"
An answering voice was heard,—it spake to me,—
God spake from heaven—"This judgment shall not be."

Soon, nature's languid form, reviving fair,
Sang praises to the God who answers prayer;—
Vanish'd the reptile host,—the withering stem
Spread forth anew, the bud reveal'd its gem,—
Deep mourning earth, her robe of joy resum'd,
And spicy gums, the summer gales perfum'd.

A flame!—a flame!—its awful ravage spread
With quenchless wrath and indignation dread,
Fed on the domes of pride, with angry sweep
And hiss'd defiance at the watery deep.
Ah!—who shall stay its rage, or curb its power?
Our God!—protect us,—in this dreadful hour.

Long in my midnight prayer, I wept and mourn'd,—
"This also shall not be,"—Jehovah's voice return'd.

Repent! Repent!—ye rebel race, I cried,—
Go mourn and seek your God, ye sons of pride.
Ye wound the stranger,—on the poor ye press,—
Defraud the widow and the fatherless,—
Ye scoff at justice,—every sin ye know,—
And give to idols what to God ye owe.
Scorn and contempt upon his law ye cast,—
And think ye to escape his righteous wrath at last?

Your palace shakes!—A sword in crimson dy'd,
Is drawn, all reeking, from your prince's side,—
Hoarse cries of treason rend the shuddering air,—
Murder and strife, and foul revolt are there,—
Woes tread on woes, and trembling pity weeps
O'er your fall'n city and its slaughter'd heaps.

Ho!—ye, who sink on couches, soft with down,—
And all your crimes in wine and music drown,—
Who snatch the garment from the shivering poor,
And wrest his pittance, to increase your store,—

You, first, the plagues and wants of war shall
vex,
The captive's yoke shall cling around your
necks,
And you shall groan, in servitude and scorn,
Like the slave sorrowing o'er his dead first-born.
Ah sinful nation!—of thy God accurst,
Thy glory stain'd, thy crown defil'd with dust,
Go,—hide thee in Mount Carmel,—dive the
deep,—
Plunge in the slimy cells where serpents creep,—
Make through the earth's dark dens, thy secret
path,—
Yet canst thou shun the purpose of His wrath?

"Hence, to your woods," they cried, "your
herds and flocks,—
Go, drive your few sheep o'er the rugged
rocks,—
Who bade you dare to quit the lowing throng?
Who made you judge of violence and wrong?"

"He, who beheld me, at my humble toil,—
Content and cheerful, in my native soil,—
He, who beholds you, from the frowning skies,—
And all your wrath and arrogance defies;—
He call'd me from my flocks and pastures fair,
He gave the message, which I boldly bear,—
And which I bear till death:—so breathe your ire,
And wreak such vengeance, as your souls de-
sire.

Say,—whose strong arm compos'd this wondrous frame?
Who stay'd the fury of the rushing flame?
Who made the mighty sun to know his place?
And fill'd with countless orbs yon concave space?
Who from his cistern bade the waters flow
And on the spent cloud hung his dazzling bow?
Who drives thro' realms immense his thundering car
To far Orion and the morning star?
Who light to darkness turns?—and night to death?
Gives the frail life and gathers back the breath?

Who gave this ponderous globe, with nicest care
To balance lightly on the fluid air?
Who raised yon mountains to their lofty height?
Who speeds the whirlwind in its trackless flight?
Who darts thro' deep disguise, his piercing ken
To read the secret thoughts and ways of men?
Who gave the morning and the midnight birth?
Whose muffled step affrights the quaking earth?
Who curb'd the sea? and touch'd the rocks with flame?
Jehovah, God of Hosts, is his tremendous name.

DEATH OF THE PRINCIPAL OF A RETREAT FOR THE INSANE.

FEW have been mourned like thee. The wise and good
Do gather many weepers round their tomb,
And true affection makes her heart an urn
For the departed idol, till that heart
Is ashes. With such sorrow art thou mourned,
And more than this. There is a cry of woe
Within the halls of yon majestic dome—
A tide of grief, which reason may not check,
Nor faith's deep anchor fathom.
Straining eyes
That gaze on vacancy, do search for thee,
Whose wand could put to flight the fancied ills
Of sick imagination. The wrecked heart
Keepeth the echo of thy soothing voice
An everlasting sigh within its cells,
And morbidly upon that music feeds.
Mind's broken column 'mid its ruins bears
Thy chiselled features. Thy dark eye looks forth

From memory's watch-tower on the phrenzy-dream,
Ruling its imagery, or with strange power
Controlling madness, as the shepherd's harp
Subdued the moody wrath of Israel's king.
Even where the links of thought and speech are broke,
'Mid that most absolute and perfect wreck,
When throneless reason flies her idiot-foe,
Thou hast a place. The fragments of the soul
Do bear thine impress—shadowy, yet endeared,
And multiplied by countless miseries.
Beside some happy hearth, where fire-side joys
And renovated health, and heaven-born hope,
Swell high in contrast with the maniac's cell,
Thou art remembered by exulting hearts,
With the deep rapture of that lunatic
Whom Jesus healed.
Still there's a wail for thee
From those poor sufferers, whom the world hath cast
Out of her company.—
Thou wert their friend,
And in their dark approach to idiocy,
Thy wasting midnight vigil was for them:
The toil, the watching, and the stifled pang
That stamped thee as a martyr, were for them.
They could not thank thee, save with that strange shriek
Which wounds the gentle ear. Yet thou didst walk

In thy high ministry of love and power,
As a magician 'mid their spectre-foes
And maniac visions.
Thou didst mark sublime
Death's angel sweeping o'er thy studious page,
And, at his chill monition, laying down
The boasted treasures of philosophy,
Enrob'd thyself in meekness as a child
Waiting the father's will.
And so farewell,
Thou full of love to all whom God hath made.
Thou tuned to melody, go home! go home!
Where music hath no dissonance, and love
Doth poise for ever on her perfect wing

LEGH RICHMOND AMONG THE RUINS OF IONA.

WHERE old Iona's ruins spread
  In shapeless fragments round,
And where the crown'd and mighty dead
  Repose in cells profound;—
Where o'er Columba's buried towers
  The shrouding ivy steals,
And moans the owl from cloister'd bowers,
  A holy teacher kneels.

Rocks spring terrific to the sky,
  Rude seas in madness storm;
And grimly frowns on Fancy's eye
  The Druid's awful form,
With mutter'd curse, and reeking blade,
  And visage stern with ire;—
Yet 'mid that darkly-blended shade
  Still bends the stranger sire.

He prays,—the father for his child
  The distant and the dear;

And where yon abbey o'er the wild
  Uprais'd its arches drear,
When at high mass, or vesper strain
  Rich voices fill'd the air,
From all that cowl'd and mitred train
  Rose there a purer prayer ?

His name is on a simple scroll
  With Christian ardour penn'd,
Which, thrilling, warns the sinner's soul
  To make his God a friend ;
But when the strong archangel's breath
  The ancient vaults shall rend,
And starting from the dust of death
  Those waken'd throngs ascend,—

Meek saint!—the boldest of the bold
  That sword or falchion drew,
Barons, whose fearful glance controll'd
  Vassal and monarch too,
Proud heroes of the tented field,
  Kings of a vaunted line,
May wish their blood-bought fame to yield
  For honours won like thine.

MARIE OF WURTEMBURG.*

Who moves in beauty, mid the regal bowers
  Of her dear native France?
And while the fairy-footed hours
  Round her all enchanted dance,
With florist's care doth nurse meek virtue's flowers?
    Who bends so low
    To hear the tale of woe,
And with a cloudless sunshine in her breast,
Findeth her highest joy, in making others blest?

  Genius, with inspiration high,
  Beams from her enkindled eye,

---

* The Princess Marie, daughter of Louis Phillippe of France, and married to Alexander, the Duke of Wurtemburg, had among other accomplishments, a great genius for sculpture. When the tidings of her death reached her native realm, the Queen said, in her grief, "I have one daughter less,—but Heaven an angel more."

Her sculptur'd touch, how fine,
The graces o'er her chisel hang, and guide its
every line.
At her creative power
Forth springs that warrior maid
Who erst in danger's darkest hour
Her country's foemen staid;
Lo! Joan of Arc, energic as of old,
Stands forth at Marie's call, and fires the marble
cold.

I hear rich music float,
Hark! 'tis a marriage lay,—
Love swells with joy the enraptur'd note,
Kings and their realms are gay,—
Bright pageants guild the auspicious day,
While Germany, who wins the gem
Thus given from Gallia's diadem,
A glad response doth pay;
And Alexander, with a princely pride,
Leads to his palace-home his all-accomplished
bride.

The skies of Italy are bright,
The olives green on Pisa's height,
But on that verdant shore
Is one whom health with rosy light
Revisiteth no more.
How sad, beneath such genial shade,
To see the flower of France reposing but to fade.

An infant's plaint of woe!
Alas, poor babe!—how dire thy fate,—
A loss thou canst not know,
Whose drear extent each opening year must show,
Meets thee at the world's fair gate:
Thy tender memory may not hold
The image of that scene of death,
When the stern spoiler, all unmov'd and cold,
Took thy sweet mother's breath,—
Thy father weeping by her side,
As, powerless on his breast, she bow'd her head and died.

She might not lull thee to thy rest,
Or longer linger here,
To dry thine infant tear,
And share the unimagin'd zest
Of young maternity.
But from her home, amid the blest,
Gazeth she not on thee?
Doth she not watch thee when soft slumbers steep
Thy gentle soul in visions deep?
Press on thy waking eyes an angel's kiss,
And bid thee rise at last, to yon pure realm of bliss?

ZAMA.

I looked, and on old Zama's arid plain
Two chieftains stood. At distance ranged their
hosts,
While they, with flashing eye, and gesture
strong,
Held their high parley. One was sternly marked
With care and hardship. Still his warrior soul
Frowned in unbroken might, as when he sealed.
In ardent boyhood, the eternal vow
Of enmity to Rome. The other seemed
Of younger years, and on his noble brow
Beauty with magnanimity sat throned;
And yet, methought, his darkening eye-ball
said,
"Delenda est Carthago."
Brief they spake,
And parted as proud souls in anger part,
While the wild shriek of trumpets, and the rush
Of cohorts rent the air. I turned away.
The pomp of battle, and the din of arms
May round a period well; but to behold

The mortal struggle, and the riven shield—
To mark how nature's holiest, tenderest ties
Are sundered—to recount the childless homes,
And sireless babes, and widows' early graves,
Made by one victor-shout, bids the blood creep
Cold through its channels.
Once again I looked—
When the pure moon unveiled a silent scene—
Silent, save when from 'neath some weltering pile
A dying war-horse neighed, in whose gored breast
Life lingered stubbornly, or some pale knight
Half-raised his arm, awakened by the call
Of his loved steed, even from the dream of death.
With stealthy step the prowling plunderer stalked,
The dark-winged raven led her clamorous brood
To their dread feast, and on the shadowy skirts
Of that dire field, the fierce hyena rolled
A keen malevolent eye.
Time sped its course,
Fresh verdure mantled Zama's fatal plain,
While Carthage, with a subjugated knee
And crownless head, toiled 'mid the slaves of Rome.

Once more I sought Hamilcar's awful son—
And, lo! an exiled, and despised old man,
Guest of Bithynian perfidy, did grasp

The poison-goblet in his withered hand,
And drink and die!
Say! is this he who rent
The bloody laurel from Saguntum's walls?
That eagle of the Alps, who through the clouds
Which wrapp'd in murky folds their slippery heights,
Goaded his ponderous elephants?—who roll'd
Victory's deep thunder o'er Ticinus' tide?
And mid the field of Cannæ wav'd his sword
Like a destroying angel?
This is he!
And this is human glory.
God of might!
Gird with Thy shield our vacillating hearts,—
That mid the illusive and bewildering paths
Of this dim pilgrimage, we may not lose
Both this world's peace, and the rewards of that
Which hath no end.
From this unmeasur'd loss,
This wreck of all probationary hope,
Defend us, Power Supreme.

PILGRIM FATHERS.

WHAT led the pilgrims through the wild
  On, to this stranger land,
Matron and maid, and fragile child,
  An uncomplaining band?
Deep streams their venturous course oppos'd,
  Dark wastes appall'd their eye;
What fill'd them on that trackless way,
  With courage bold and high?

What cheer'd them, when dire winter's wrath
  A frosty challenge threw,
And higher than their trembling roofs
  The mocking snow-drift grew?
When in its wasted mother's arms,
  To famine's ills, a prey,
The babe bereft of rosy charms
  Pin'd like a flower away?

And when the strong heart-sickness came,
  And memory's troubled stream,
Still imag'd forth fair England's homes,
  That lull'd their cradle-dream,—

When no lone vessel ploughed the wave,
  News from her clime to bear,
What nobly bore the stricken soul,
  Above that deep despair?

What gave them strength, 'mid all their toil,
  In every hour of need
To plant within this sterile soil
  A glorious nation's seed?
The same that nerv'd them when they sank
  To rest, beneath the sod,—
That rais'd o'er death, the triumph-song,—
  Prayer, and the faith of God.

"WEEP NOT."

"Weep not—he hath gone home—that little one."
MULLNER.

GONE home! Gone home!—how many a prayer
of love,
Breath'd out its ardour, to detain thee here,—
And Fancy's dream its spell of fondness wove
To make thee happy, as thou wert most dear.

Tho' round thy lip the smile complacent play'd,
And joy enwrapp'd thee in her robe of light,—
Yet was it not the *thought of home*, that made
Thy brow so beautiful?—thine eye so bright?

The thought of home! they deem'd it not, who
knew
Thy dear delight, among the garden flowers,
Thy loving heart, to warm affection true,
And all the gladness of thine infant hours.

Weep not:—'mid thornless flowers that never
fade,
In bowers of bliss where raptures never cloy,
Thou hast thy home, thy changeless mansion
made,
Our transient visitant,—our angel boy.

ON THE DEATH OF A FORMER PUPIL.

Not long it seems, since she with childish brow
Pondered her lessons,—in rich fields of thought
A ripe and ready student. Her clear mind,
Precocious, yet well-balanced,—her delight
In varied knowledge,—her melodious tone
Of elocution, falling on the ear
Like some rare harp, on which the soul doth
play,
Her sweet docility, 'twas mine to mark,—
And marking, love.
Then came the higher grades
Of woman's duty:—and the pure resolve,
The persevering goodness,—the warm growth
Of every household-charity,—the ties
That bind to earth, and yet prepare for heaven,
Were gently wreath'd amid the clustering fruits
Of ripened intellect.
But soon, alas!
In search of health, to distant scenes she turn'd,
A patient traveller, still, with wasted form,

Led on by mocking hope. And far away,
From her lov'd home, where spread in fadeless green,
The Elm, which cheer'd her sainted grandsire's gaze,
(Like Mamre's Oak, o'er Abraham's honoured head)
Far from the chamber, where her cradle rock'd,
And where she hop'd her couch of death might be
The Spoiler found her.
The long gasp was hers,—
But the meek smile was her Redeemer's gift,
His victor-token. And the bosom-friend
Took that bequest into his bursting heart,
As in the sleepless ministry of love,
He stood beside her, in that parting hour.
——See'st thou the desolate, on his return?—
Know'st thou the sadness of his lonely way?--
Deep silence, where the tender word had been,—
And at the midnight watch or trembling dawn,
The sullen echo of the hearse-like wheel,
Avoiding every haunt, and pleasant bower
Where the dear invalid so late reclin'd,
Lest some light question of a stranger's tongue
Should harrow up the soul. Know'st thou the pang
When his reft home, first met his mournful view?
——What brings he to his children?——

Yon fair boy
Who at the casement stands and weeps,—can
tell,—
And he, who cannot tell,—that younger one,
Whose boundless loss steals like some strange
eclipse
Over a joyous planet,—and the babe
Stretching its arms for her who comes no more.
Oh! if the blest in heaven, take note of earth,
Will not the mother's hovering spirit brood
O'er those fair boys?
It is not ours to say,—
We only know that if a christian's faith
Hath changeless promise of the life to come,
That heritage is hers. And so we lay
Her body in the tomb,—with praise to God
For her example,—and with prayer, to close
Our time of trial, in such trust serene.

THE SLEEPING INFANT.

Sweet infant, beautiful as light,
 That on the snow-drop's bosom glows,
When scap'd from wrathful winter's might,
 It trembles through incumbent snows,—

Amid thy cradle sleep we watch
 The varying thought that faintly gleams,
As tho' we fondly hop'd to catch
 The angel-whisper of thy dreams.

The angel-whisper. Tell us what
 Is breath'd from that celestial clime;
Thou, nearer to its white-winged host
 Than we who tread the thorns of time:—

Thou canst not tell,—no words are thine,—
 But the pure smile that lights thy brow
Is sure the language of the skies,—
 Oh keep it still unchanged—as now.

THE ORPHAN'S TRUST.

"When my father and my mother forsake me, then the Lord will take me up."—DAVID.

HE, who around my infant steps,
  A firm protection threw,
Whose prayers upon my head distill'd,
  Like summer's holy dew,—
The staff hath fallen from his hand,
  The mantle from his breast,
And underneath the church-yard mould
  He takes a quiet rest.

And she, who at each cradle-moan,
  At every childish tear,
At every fleeting trace of pain
  Stood, full of pity near;—
Who to her fondly-cherish'd child
  Such deep affection bore,
She too, hath given the parting kiss,
  And must return no more.

And therefore, unto Thee I turn,
  The never-changing Friend,
Whose years eternal cannot fail,
  Whose mercies have no end ;—
Thro' all my pilgrim path below,
  A Father deign to be,
And show that mother's tender love
  Who hath forsaken me.

THE ORDINATION.

Up to thy Master's work! for thou art sworn
To do his bidding, till the hand of death
Strike off thine armour. Thy deep vow denies
To hoard earth's gold, or truckle for its smile,
Or bind its blood-stain'd laurel on thy brow.

-A nobler field is thine.—The soul! the soul!—
That is thy province,—that mysterious thing,
Which hath no limit from the walls of sense,—
No chill from hoary time,—with pale decay
No fellowship,—but shall stand forth unchang'd,
Unscath'd amid the resurrection fires,
To bear its boundless lot of good or ill.
And dost thou take authority to aid
This pilgrim-essence to a throne in heaven
Among the glorious harpers, and the ranks
Of radiant seraphim and cherubim?

Thy business is with that which cannot die,—
Whose subtle thought the untravell'd universe

Spans on swift wing, from slumbering ages sweeps
Their buried treasures, scans the vault of heaven,
Poises the orbs of light, points boldly out
Their trackless pathway through the blue expanse,
Foils the red comet in its flaming speed,
And aims to read the secrets of its God.
—Yet thou, a son of clay, art privileg'd
To make thy Saviour's image brighter stil.
In this majestic soul!

Give God the praise
That thou art counted worthy,—and lay down
Thy lip in dust.—Bethink thee of its loss,
For He whose sighs on Olivet, whose pangs
On Calvary, best speak its priceless worth,
Saith that it may be lost. Should it sin on
Till the last hour of grace and penitence
Is meted out, ah! what would it avail
Though the whole world, with all its pomp, and power,
And plumage, were its own? What were its gain
If the brief hour-glass of this life should fail,
And leave remorse no grave,—despair, no hope?

Up, blow thy trumpet, sound the loud alarm
To those who sleep in Zion. Boldly warn
To 'scape their condemnation, o'er whose head

Age after age of misery hath roll'd,
Who from their prison-house look up and see
Heaven's golden gate, and to its watchmen cry,
"What of the night?" while the dread answer falls
With fearful echo down the unfathom'd depths:
"Eternity!"
Should one of those lost souls
Amid its tossings utter forth thy name,
As one who might have pluck'd it from the pit,
Thou man of God! would there not be a burst
Of tears in heaven?
O, live the life of prayer,
The life of faith in the meek Son of God,
The life of tireless labour for His sake:
So may the angel of the covenant, bring
Thee to thy home in bliss, with many a gem
To glow for ever in thy Master's crown.

THE HOST OF GIDEON.

Of the crystal stream.et taste,
Warriors, in your eager haste,—
Here refresh your wearied line,
Ere in battle-strife ye join.
—Some upon the verdant strand
Scoop the water with their hand,
Others, on their knees supine,
For a deeper draught incline.
—But their chieftain standing by,
Mark'd them with an eagle-eye,
And his heaving bosom fir'd,
As he spake the doom inspir'd.
"By the few, who scoop'd the wave,
Shall our God, his Israel save,—
On,—ye chosen,—on with me,—
Yours the toil,—the victory."
Small the band, yet on they prest
Heaven's own courage in their breast,
And the strong and haughty foe,
Covering all the vale below,—
At their onset hold and high,
At their trumpet's fearful cry.

Prince, and chariot, turn'd and fled,
Helpless in that hour of dread.
  Soldiers of a glorious head,
While this leagur'd earth ye tread,
Lightly taste of Pleasure's wave,—
Bow not down like Passion's slave,
Lest, while others watchful stand,
Ye forget the promis'd land,
Lest, thy Leader's voice decree
Joy to them, and shame to thee.

FAREWELL.

Farewell! it hath a sombre tone,
  The lip is slow to take it,
It seemeth like the willow's moan
  When autumn winds awake it:
It seemeth like the distant sea
  Round some lone islet sighing,
And yet thou say'st it unto me,
  And wait'st for my replying.

Farewell! thou fly'st from Winter's wrath
  'Mid sunny bowers to hide thee,
May freshest roses deck thy path,
  Yet bring no thorn to chide thee;
And may'st thou find that better land
  Where no bright dream is broken,
No flower shall fade in beauty's hand,
  And no farewell be spoken.

THE DREAM.

'Twas summer eve; the changeful beams still
play'd
On the fir-bark and through the beechen shade;
Still with soft crimson glow'd each floating cloud,
Still the stream glitter'd where the willow bow'd
Still the pale moon sate silent and alone,
Nor yet the stars had rallied round her throne;
Those diamond courtiers, who, while yet the
West
Wears the red shield above his dying breast,
Dare not assume the loss they all desire,
Nor pay their homage to the fainter fire,
But wait in trembling till the Sun's fair light
Fading, shall leave them free to welcome night!

So when some Chief, whose name through
realms afar
Was still the watchword of successful war,
Met by the fatal hour which waits for all,
Is, on the field he rallied, forced to fall,
The conquerors pause to watch his parting
breath,
Awed by the terrors of that mighty death:

Nor dared the meed of victory to claim,
Nor lift the standard to a meaner name,
Till every spark of soul hath ebb'd away,
And leaves what was a hero, common clay.

Oh! Twilight! Spirit that dost render birth
To dim enchantments; melting Heaven with
Earth,
Leaving on craggy hills and running streams
A softness like the atmosphere of dreams;
Thy hour to all is welcome! Faint and sweet
Thy light falls round the peasant's homeward
feet,
Who, slow returning from his task of toil,
Sees the low sunset gild the cultured soil,
And, tho' such radiance round him brightly
glows,
Marks the small spark his cottage window
throws.
Still as his heart forestals his weary pace,
Fondly he dreams of each familiar face,
Recalls the treasures of his narrow life,
His rosy children, and his sunburnt wife,
To whom *his* coming is the chief event
Of simple days in cheerful labor spent.
The rich man's chariot hath gone whirling past,
And those poor cottagers have only cast
One careless glance on all that show of pride,
Then to their tasks turn'd quietly aside;
But *him* they wait for, him they welcome home,
Fond sentinels look forth to see him come;
The fagot sent for when the fire grew dim,

The frugal meal prepared, are all for him ;
For him the watching of that sturdy boy
For him those smiles of tenderness and joy,
For him,—who plods his sauntering way along,
Whistling the fragment of some village song!

Dear art thou to the lover, thou sweet light,
Fair fleeting sister of the mournful night!
As in impatient hope he stands apart,
Companion'd only by his beating heart,
And with an eager fancy oft beholds
The vision of a white robe's fluttering folds
Flit through the grove, and gain the open mead,
True to the hour by loving hearts agreed!
At length she comes. The evening's holy grace
Mellows the glory of her radiant face ;
The curtain of that daylight faint and pale
Hangs round her like the shrouding of a veil;
As, turning with a bashful timid thought,
From the dear welcome she herself hath sought,
Her shadowy profile drawn against the sky
Cheats, while it charms, his fond adoring eye.

Oh! dear to him, to all, since first the flowers
Of happy Eden's consecrated bowers
Heard the low breeze along the branches play,
And God's voice bless the cool hour of the day.
For though that glorious Paradise be lost,
Though earth by blighting storms be roughly
cross'd,
Though the long curse demands the tax of sin
And the day's sorrows with the day begin,

That hour, once sacred to God's presence, still
Keeps itself calmer from the touch of ill,
The holiest hour of Earth. *Then* toil doth
cease—
Then from the yoke the oxen find release—
Then man rests pausing from his many cares,
And the world teems with children's sunset
prayers!
Then innocent things seek out their natural rest,
The babe sinks slumbering on its mother's
breast;
The birds beneath their leafy covering creep,
Yea, even the flowers fold up their buds in sleep;
And angels, floating by, on radiant wings,
Hear the low sound the breeze of evening brings,
Catch the sweet incense as it floats along,
The infant's prayer, the mother's cradle-song,
And bear the holy gifts to worlds afar,
As things too sacred for this fallen star.

At such an hour, on such a summer night,
Silent and calm in its transparent light,
A widow'd parent watch'd her slumbering child,
On whose young face the sixteenth summer
smiled.
Fair was the face she watch'd! Nor less,
because
Beauty's perfection seemed to make a pause,
And wait, on that smooth brow, some further
touch,
Some spell from time,—the great magician,—
such

As calls the closed bud out of hidden gloom,
And bids it wake to glory, light and bloom.
Girlish as yet, but with the gentle grace
Of a young fawn in its low resting-place,
Her folded limbs were lying: from her hand
A group of wild flowers—Nature's brightest band,
Of all that laugh along the summer fields,
Of all the sunny hedge-row freely yields,
Of all that in the wild-wood darkly hide,
Or on the thyme-bank wave in breezy pride,—
Show'd that the weariness which closed in sleep
So tranquil, child-like, innocent, and deep,
Nor festal gaiety, nor toilsome hours,
Had brought; but, like a flower among the flowers,
She had been wandering 'neath a summer sky,
Youth on her lip and gladness in her eye,
Twisting the wild rose from its native thorn,
And the blue scabious from the sunny corn;
Smiling and singing like a spirit fair
That walk'd the world, but had no dwelling there.
And still (as though their faintly-scented breath
Preserv'd a meek fidelity in death)
Each late imprison'd blossom fondly lingers
Within the touch of her unconscious fingers,
Though, languidly unclasp'd, that hand no more
Guards its possession of the rifled store.

So wearily she lay; so sweetly slept;
So by her side fond watch the mother kept;

And, as above her gentle child she bent,
So like they seem'd in form and lineament,
You might have deem'd her face its shadow gave
To the clear mirror of a fountain's wave;
Only in this they differ'd; that, while one
Was warm and radiant as the summer sun,
The other's smile had more a moonlight play
For many tears had wept its glow away;
Yet was she fair; of loveliness so true,
That time, which faded, never could subdue;
And though the sleeper, like a half-blown rose
Show'd bright as angels in her soft repose,
Though bluer veins ran through each snowy lid,
Curtaining sweet eyes, by long dark lashes hid—
Eyes that as yet had never learnt to weep,
But woke up smiling, like a child's, from sleep;—
Though fainter lines were pencill'd on the brow,
Which cast soft shadow on the orbs below;
Though deeper color flush'd her youthful cheek,
In its smooth curve more joyous and less meek,
And fuller seem'd the small and crimson mouth,
With teeth like those that glitter in the south—
She had but youth's superior brightness, such
As the skill'd painter gives with flattering touch
When he would picture every lingering grace
Which once shone brighter in some copied face;
And it was compliment, whene'er she smiled,
To say, "Thou'rt like thy mother, my fair child!"

Sweet is the image of the brooding dove!—
Holy as Heaven a mother's tender love!
The love of many prayers and many tears,
Which changes not with dim declining years—
The *only* love which on this teeming earth
Asks no return from Passion's wayward birth;
The only love that, with a touch divine,
Displaces from the heart's most secret shrine
The idol Self. Oh! prized beneath thy due
When life's untried affections all are new—
Love, from whose calmer hope and holier rest
(Like a fledged bird, impatient of the nest)
The human heart, rebellious, springs to seek
Delights more vehement, in ties more weak;
How strange to us appears, in after-life,
That term of mingled carelessness and strife,
When guardianship so gentle gall'd our pride,
When it was holiday to leave thy side,
When, with dull ignorance that *would not* learn,
We lost those hours that never can return—
Hours, whose most sweet communion Nature meant
Should be in confidence and kindness spent,
That we (hereafter mourning) might believe
In human faith, though all around deceive;
Might weigh against the sad and startling crowd
Of ills which wound the weak and chill the proud,
Of woes 'neath which (despite of stubborn will,
Philosophy's vain boast, and erring skill)
The strong heart downward like a willow bends,
Failure of love,—and treachery of friends,—
Our recollections of the undefiled,

The sainted tie, of parent and of child!
Oh! happy days! Oh years that glided by,
Scarce chronicled by one poor passing sigh!
When the dark storm sweeps past us, and the soul
Struggles with fainting strength to reach the goal;
When the false baits that lured us only cloy,
What would we give to grasp your vanish'd joy!
From the cold quicksands of Life's treacherous shore
The backward light our anxious eyes explore,
Measure the miles our wandering feet have come,
Sinking heart-weary, far away from home,
Recall the voice that whisper'd love and peace
The smile that bid our early sorrows cease,
And long to bow our grieving heads, and weep
Low on the gentle breast that lull'd us first to sleep!

Ah! bless'd are they for whom 'mid all their pains
That faithful and unalter'd love remains;
Who, Life wreck'd round them,—hunted from their rest,—
And, by all else forsaken or distress'd,—
Claim, in *one* heart, their sanctuary and shrine—
As I, my Mother, claim'd my place in thine!

Oft, since that hour, in sadness I retrace
My childhood's vision of thy calm sweet face

Oft see thy form, its mournful beauty shrouded
  In thy black weeds, and coif of widow's woe;
Thy dark expressive eyes all dim and clouded
  By that deep wretchedness the lonely know:
Stifling thy grief, to hear some weary task
  Conn'd by unwilling lips, with listless air,
Hoarding thy means, lest future need might ask
  More than the widow's pittance then could spare.
Hidden, forgotten by the great and gay,
  Enduring sorrow, not by fits and starts,
But the long self-denial, day by day,
  Alone amidst thy brood of careless hearts!
Striving to guide, to teach, or to restrain,
  The young rebellious spirits crowding round,
Who saw not, knew not, felt not for thy pain,
  And could not comfort—yet had power to wound!
Ah! how my selfish heart, which since hath grown
Familiar with deep trials of its own,
With riper judgment looking to the past,
Regrets the careless days that flew so fast,
Stamps with remorse each wasted hour of time,
And darkens every folly into crime!

Warriors and statesmen have their meed of praise,
  And what they do or suffer men record;
But the long sacrifice of woman's days
  Passes without a thought—without a word;
And many a holy struggle for the sake

Of duties sternly, faithfully fulfill'd—
For which the anxious mind must watch and wake,
And the strong feelings of the heart be still'd,—
Goes by unheeded as the summer wind,
And leaves no memory and no trace behind!
Yet, it may be, more lofty courage dwells
In one meek heart which braves an adverse fate,
Than his, whose ardent soul indignant swells
Warm'd by the fight, or cheer'd through high debate:
The Soldier dies surrounded; could he *live*
Alone to suffer, and alone to strive?

Answer, ye graves, whose suicidal gloom
Shows deeper horror than a common tomb!
Who sleep within? The men who would evade
An unseen lot of which they felt afraid.
Embarrassment of means, which work'd annoy,—
A past remorse,—a future blank of joy,—
The sinful rashness of a blank despair,—
These were the strokes which sent your victims there.

In many a village churchyard's simple grave,
Where all unmark'd the cypress branches wave
In many a vault where Death could only claim,
The brief inscription of a woman's name;
Of different ranks, and different degrees,
From daily labor to a life of ease.

(From the rich wife who through the weary day
Wept in her jewels, grief's unceasing prey,
To the poor soul who trudged o'er marsh and
moor,
And with her baby begg'd from door to door,—)
Lie hearts, which, ere they found that last
release,
Had lost all memory of the blessing "Peace;'
Hearts, whose long struggle through unpitied
years
None saw but Him who marks the mourner's
tears;
The obscurely noble! who evaded not
The woe which He had will'd should be their
lot,
But nerved themselves to bear!

Of such art thou,
My Mother! With thy calm and holy brow,
And high devoted heart, which suffer'd still
Unmurmuring, through each degree of ill.
And, because Fate hath will'd that mine should
be
A Poet's soul (at least in my degree,)—
And that my verse would faintly shadow forth
What I have seen of pure unselfish worth,—
Therefore I speak of Thee; that those who read
That trust in woman, which is still my creed,
Thy early-widow'd image may recall
And greet thy nature as the type of all!

Enough! With eyes of fond unwearied love
The Mother of my story watch'd above

Her sleeping child; and, as she views the grace
And blushing beauty of that girlish face,
Her thoughts roam back through change of time and tide,
Since first Heaven sent the blessing by her side.

In that sweet vision she again receives
The snow-white cradle, where that tiny head
Lay, like a small bud folded in its leaves,
Foster'd with dew by tears of fondness shed;
Each infantine event, each dangerous hour
Which pass'd with threatening o'er its fragile form,
Her hope, her anguish, as the tender flower
Bloom'd to the sun, or sicken'd in the storm,
In memory's magic mirror glide along,
And scarce she notes the different scene around,
And scarce her lips refrain the cradle-song
Which sooth'd that infant with its lulling sound!
But the dream changes; quiet years roll on;
That dawn of frail existence fleets away,
And she beholds beneath the summer sun
A blessed sight; a little child at play.
The soft light falls upon its golden hair,
And shows a brow intelligently mild;
No more a cipher in this world of care,
Love cheers and chides that happy conscious child.
No more unheeding of her watchful love,
Pride to excel, its docile spirit stirs;

Regret and hope its tiny bosom move,
  And looks of fondness brightly answer hers;
O'er the green meadow, and the broomy hill,
  In restless joy it bounds and darts along;
Or through the breath of evening, low and still,
  Carols with mirthful voice its welcome song.

Again the vision changes; from her view
  The CHILD's dear love and antic mirth are gone;
But, in their stead, with cheek of rose-leaf hue,
  And fair slight form, and low and silvery tone,
Rises the sweetest spirit Thought can call
  From memory's distant worlds—the fairy GIRL;
Whose heart her childish pleasures still enthrall,
  Whose unbound hair still floats in careless curl,
But in whose blue and meekly lifted eyes,
  And in whose shy, though sweet and cordial smile,
And in whose changeful blushes, dimly rise
  Shadows and lights that were not seen erewhile:
Shadows and lights that speak of woman's love,
  Of all that makes or mars her fate below;
Mysterious prophecies, which Time must prove
  More bright in glory, or more dark with woe!
And that soft vision also wanders by,
  Melting in fond and innocent smiles away,
Till the loved REAL meets the watchful eye
  Of her who thus recall'd a former day;
The gentle daughter, for whose precious sake

Her widow'd heart had struggled with its pain,
And still through lonely grief refused to break,
Because *that* tie to Earth did yet remain.
Now, as she fondly gazed, a few meek tears
Stole down her cheek; for she that slumber'd there,
The beautiful, the loved of many years,
A bride betroth'd must leave her fostering care;
Woo'd in another's home apart to dwell—
Oh! might that other love but half as well!
As if the mournful wish had touch'd her heart,
The slumbering maiden woke, with sudden start;
Turn'd, with a dazzled and intense surprise,
On that fond face her bright, bewilder'd eyes;
Gazed round on each familiar object near,
As though she doubted yet if sense was clear,
Cover'd her brow and sigh'd, as though to wake
Had power some spell of happy thought to break;
Then murmur'd, in a low and earnest tone,
"Oh! is that blessed dream for ever gone?"

Strange is the power of dreams! Who hath not felt,
When in the light such visions melt,
How the veil'd soul, though struggling to be free,
Ruled by that deep unfathom'd mystery,
Wakes, haunted by the thoughts of good or ill
Whose shadowy influence pursues us still?

Sometimes romorse doth weigh our spirits down;
Some crime committed earns Heaven's angriest frown;
Some awful sin, in which the tempted heart
Hath scarce, perhaps, forborne its waking part,
Brings dreams of judgment; loud the thunders roll,
The heavens shrink blacken'd like a flaming scroll;
We faint, we die, beneath the avenging rod,
And vainly hide from our offended God.
For oh! though fancy change our mortal lot,
And rule our slumbers, CONSCIENCE sleepeth not;
That strange sad dial, by its own true light,
Points to our thoughts, how dark soe'er the night,
Still by our pillow watchful guard it keeps,
And bids the sinner tremble while he sleeps.

Sometimes, with fearful dangers doom'd to cope,
'Reft of each wild and visionary hope,
Stabb'd with a thousand wounds, we struggle still,
The hand that tortures, powerless to kill.
Sometimes 'mid ocean storms, in fearful strife,
We stem the wave, and shrieking, gasp for life,
While crowding round us, faces rise and gleam,
Some known and loved, some, pictures of our dream

High on the buoyant waters wildly toss'd—
Low in its foaming caverns darkly lost—
Those flitting forms the dangerous hour partake,
Cling to our aid, or suffer for our sake.
Conscious of present life, the slumbering soul
Still floats us onward, as the billows roll,
Till, snatch'd from death, we seem to touch the strand,
Rise on the shoreward wave, and dash to land!
Alone we come: the forms whose wild array
Gleam'd round us while we struggled, fade away—
We know not, reck not, who the danger shared,
But, vaguely dreaming, feel that *we* are spared.

Sometimes a grief, of fond affection born,
Gnaws at our heart, and bids us weep till morn;
Some anguish, copied from our waking fears,
Wakes the eternal fount of human tears,
Sends us to watch some vision'd bed of death,
Hold the faint hand, and catch the parting breath,
Where those we prized the most, and loved the best,
Seem darkly sinking to the grave's long rest;
Lo! in our arms they fade, they faint, they die,
Before our eyes the funeral train sweeps by!
We hear the orphan's sob—the widow's wail—
O'er our dim senses woeful thoughts prevail,
Till, with a burst of grief, the spell we break,
And, weeping for th' imagined loss, awake.
Ah me! from dreams like these aroused at length,

How leaps the spirit to its former strength!
What memories crowd the newly conscious brain,
What gleams of rapture, and what starts of pain!
Till from the soul the heavy mists stand clear,
All wanes and fades that seem'd so darkly drear
The sun's fair rays those shades of death destroy,
And passionate thankfulness and tears of joy
Swell at our hearts, as, gazing on his beam,
We start, and cry aloud, "Thank Heaven 'twas but a dream!"

But there are visions of a fairer kind,
Thoughts fondly cherish'd by the slumbering mind,
Which, when they vanish from the waking brain,
We close our eyes, and long to dream again.
Their dim voice calls to our forsaken side
Those who betray'd us, seeming true and tried ·
Those whom the fast receding waves of time
Have floated from us; those who in the prime
And glory of our young life's eagle flight
Shone round like rays, encircling us with light,
And gave the bright similitude of truth
To fair illusions—vanish'd with our youth.
They bring again the tryst of early love,
(That passionate hope, all other hopes above!)
Bid the pale hair, long shrouded in the grave,
Round the young head in floating ringlets wave,
And fill the air with echoes. Gentle words,
Low laughter, and the singing of sweet birds,

Come round us then; and dropping of light
boughs,
Whose shadow could not cool our burning brows,
And lilac-blossoms, scenting the warm air,
And long laburnums, fragile, bright, and fair;
And murmuring breezes through the green
leaves straying,
And rippling waters in the sunshine playing,
All that around our slumbering sense can fling
The glory of some half-forgotten spring!
They bring again the fond approving gaze
Of old true friends, who mingled love with
praise;
When Fame (that cold bright guiding-star be-
low)
Took from affection's light a borrow'd glow—
And, strong in all the might of earnest thought,
Through the long studious night untired we
wrought,
That others might the morning hours beguile,
With the fond triumph of their wondering smile.
What though those dear approving smiles be
gone,
What though we strive neglected and alone,
What though no voice *now* mourns our hope's
alloy,
Nor in that hour of triumph gives us joy?
In *dreams* the days return when this was not,
When strong affection sooth'd our toilsome lot;
Cheer'd, loved, admonish'd, lauded, we aspire,
And the sick soul regains its former fire.

Beneath the influence of this fond spell,
Happy, contented, bless'd, we seem to dwell;
Sweet faces shine with love's own tender ray,
Which frown, or coldly turn from us, by day;
The lonely orphan hears a parent's voice;
Sad childless mothers once again rejoice;
The poor deserted seems a happy bride;
And the long parted wander side by side.

Ah, vain deceit; Awakening with a start,
Sick grows the beatings of the troubled heart;
Silence, like some dark mantle, drops around,
Quenching th' imagined voice's welcome sound,
Again the soul repeats its old farewells,
Again recalls sad hours and funeral knells;
Again, as daylight opens on their view,
The orphan shrinks, the mother mourns anew;
Till clear we feel, as fades the morning star,
How left, how lonely, how oppress'd we are!

And other dreams exist, more vague and bright
Than MEMORY ever brought to cheer the night;—
Most to the young and happy do they come,
To those who know no shelter but of home;
To those of whom the inspired writer spoke,
When from his lips the words prophetic broke,
Which (conscious of the strong and credulous spell
Experience only in the heart can quell)
Promised the nearer glimpse of perfect truth
Not to cold wisdom but to fervent youth

Each, in their measure, caught its fitful gleams—
The young saw visions, and the old dream'd dreams.

The young! Oh! what should wandering fancy bring
In life's first spring-time but the thoughts of spring?
World without winter, blooming amaranth bowers,
Garlands of brightness wreath'd from changeless flowers;
Where shapes like angels wander to and fro,
Unwing'd, but glorious, in the noontide glow,
Which steeps the hills, the dales, the earth, the sea,
In one soft flood of golden majesty.
In this world,—so create,—no sighs nor tears,—
No sadness brought with lapse of varying years,—
No cold betrayal of the trusting heart,—
No knitting up of love fore-doom'd to part —
No pain, deformity, nor pale disease,—
No wars,—no tyranny,—nor fears that freeze
The rapid current of the restless blood,—
Nor effort scorn'd,—nor act misunderstood,—
No dark remorse for ever-haunting sin,—
But all at peace without,—at rest within,
And hopes which gild Thought's wildest waking hours,
Scatter'd around us carelessly as flowers.

Oh! Paradise, in vain didst thou depart•
Thine image still is stamp'd on every heart!

Though mourning man in vain may seek to trace
The site of that which *was* his dwelling-place,
Though the four glittering rivers *now* divide
No realms of beauty with their rolling tide.
Each several life yet opens with the view
Of that unblighted world where Adam drew
The breath of being: in each several mind,
However cramp'd, and fetter'd, and confined,
The innate power of beauty folded lies,
And, like a bud beneath the summer skies,
Blooms out in youth through many a radiant day
Though in life's winter frost it dies away.

From such a vision, bright with all the fame
Her youth, her innocence, her hope could frame
The maiden woke: and, when her shadowy gaze
Had lost the dazzled look of wild amaze
Turn'd on her mother when she first awoke,
Thus to her questioning glance she answering spoke:—

"Methought, oh! gentle Mother, by thy side
I dwelt no more as now, but through a wide
And sweet world wander'd; nor even then alone;
For ever in that dream's soft light stood one,
I know not who,—yet most familiar seem'd
The fond companionship of which I dream'd;
A Brother's love, is but a name to me;
A Father's brighten'd not my infancy;
To me in childhood's years, no stranger's face
Took, from long habit, friendship's holy grace
3

My life hath still been lone, and needed not,
Heaven knows, more perfect love than was my
lot,
In thy dear heart: how dream'd I then, sweet
Mother,
Of any love but thine, who knew no other?

"We seem'd, this shadow and myself, to be
Together by the blue and boundless sea;
No settled home was present to my thought—
No other form my clouded fancy brought;
This one Familiar Presence still beguiled
My every thought, and look'd on me and smiled.
Fair stretch'd in beauty lay the glittering strand,
With low green copses sloping from the land;
And tangled underwood and sunny fern,
And flowers whose humble names none cared
to learn,
Small starry wild flowers, white and gold and
blue,
With leaves turn'd crimson by the autumual hue,
Bask'd in the fervor of the noontide glow,
Whose hot rays pierced the thirsty roots below,
The floating nautilus rose clear and pale,
As though a spirit trimm'd its fairy sail,
White and transparent; and beyond it gleam'd
Such light as never yet on Ocean beam'd:
And pink-lipp'd shells, and many color'd weeds,
And long brown bulbous things like jaspar beads,
And glistening pearls in beauty faint and fair,
And all things strange, and wonderful, and rare,
Whose true existence travellers make known,

Seem'd scatter'd there, and easily my own.
And then we wove our ciphers in the sands,
All fondly intertwined by loving hands;
And laugh'd to see the rustling snow-white spray
Creep o'er the names, and wash their trace away.
And the storm came not, though the white foam curl'd
In lines of brightness far along the coast;
Though many a ship, with swelling sails unfurl'd,
From the mid-sea to sheltering haven cross'd;
Though the wild billows heaved, and rose, and broke,
One o'er the other with a restless sound,
And the deep spirit of the wind awoke,
Ruffling in wrath each glassy verdant mound
While onward roll'd that army of huge waves,
Until the foremost, with exulting roar,
Rose, proudly crested, o'er his brother slaves,
And dash'd triumphant on the groaning shore
For then the Moon rose up, Night's mournful Queen,
'Walking with white feet o'er the troubled Sea,'
And all grew still again, as she had been
Heaven's messenger to bring Tranquility;
Till, pale and tender, on the glistening main
She sank and smiled like one who loves in vain.
And still we linger'd by that shadowy strand,
Happy, yet full of thought, hand link'd in hand,

The hush'd waves rippling softly at our feet,
The night-breeze freshening o'er the summer's
heat;
With our hearts beating, and our gazing eyes
Fix'd on the star-light of those deep blue skies,
Blessing 'the year, the hour, the place the
time;'
While sounded, faint and far, some turret's
midnight chime.

"It pass'd, that vision of the Ocean's might!
I know not how, for in my slumbering mind
There was no movement, all was shifting light,
Through which we floated with the wander-
ing wind;
And, still together, in a different scene,
We look'd on England's woodland, fresh and
green.

"No perfume of the cultured rose was there,
Wooing the senses with its garden smell,—
Nor snow-white lily,—called so proudly fair,
Though by the poor man's cot she loves to
dwell,
Nor finds his little garden scant of room
To bid her stately buds in beauty bloom;—
Nor jasmin, with her pale stars shining through
The myrtle darkness of her leaf's green hue,—
Nor helitrope, whose gray and heavy wreath
Mimics the orchard blossoms' fruity breath—
Nor clustering dahlia, with its scentless flower

Cheating the heart through autumn's faded hours,—
Nor bright chrysanthimum, whose train'd array
Still makes the rich man's winter path look gay,
And bows its hardy head when wild winds blow,
To free its petals from the fallen snow;—
Nor yet carnation;"—

(Thou, beloved of all
The plants that thrive at Art or Nature's call,
By one who greets thee with a weary sigh
As the dear friend of happy days gone by;
By one who names thee last, but loves thee first,
Of all the flowers a garden ever nursed;
The mute remembrancer and gentle token
Of links which heavy hands have roughly broken,
Welcomed through many a Summer with the same
Unalter'd gladness as when first ye came,
And welcomed still, though—as in later years
We often welcome pleasant things—with tears!

I wander! In the Dream these had no place—
Nor Sorrow:—all was Nature's freshest grace.

"There, wild geranium, with its woolly stem
And aromatic breath, perfumed the glade;
And fairy speedwell, like some sapphire gem,
Lighted with purple sparks the hedge-row's shade;
And woodbine, with her tinted calyxes,

And dog-rose glistening with the dews of morn,
And tangled wreaths of tufted clematis,
Whose blossoms pale the careless eye may scorn,
As green and light her fairy mantles fall
To hide the rough hedge or the crumbling wall.
But in whose breast the laden wild-bees dive
For the best riches of their teeming hive:
"There, sprang the sunny cricket; there, was spread
The fragile silver of the spider's thread,
Stretching from blade to blade of emerald grass,
Unbroken, till some human footstep pass;
There, by the rippling stream that murmur'd on,
Now seen, now hidden—half in light, half Sun—
The darting dragon-fly, with sudden gleam,
Shot, as it went, a gold and purple beam;
And the fish leap'd within the deeper pool,
And the green trees stretch'd out their branches cool,
Where many a bird hush'd in her peopled nest
The unfledged darlings of her feather'd breast,
Listening her mate's clear song, in that sweet grove
Where all around breathed happiness and love!

"And while we talk'd the summer hours flew fast,
As hours may fly, with those whose love is young;
Who fear no future, and who know no past

Dating existence from the hope that sprung
Up in their hearts with such a sudden light,
That all beyond shows dark and blank as night.
' Until methought we trod a wide flat heath,
Where yew and cypress darkly seem'd to wave
O'er countless tombs, so beautiful, that death
Seem'd here to make a garden of the grave!
All that is holy, tender, full of grace,
Was sculptured on the monuments around,
And many a line the musing eye could trace,
Which spoke unto the heart without a sound.
There lay the warrior and the son of song,
And there—in silence till the judgment-day—
The orator, whose all-persuading tongue
Had moved the nations with resistless sway
There slept pale men whom science taught to climb
Restlessly upward all their laboring youth;
Who left, half conquer'd, secrets which in time
Burst on mankind in ripe and glorious truth.
He that had gazed upon the steadfast stars,
And could foretell the dark eclipse's birth,
And when red comets in their blazing cars
Should sweep above the awed and troubled earth:—
He that had sped brave vessels o'er the seas,
Which swiftly bring the wanderer to his home,
Uncanvass'd ships, which move without a breeze,
Their bright wheels dashing through the ocean foam:—

All, who in this life's bounded brief career
  Had shone amongst or served their fellow
    men,
And left a name embalm'd in glory here,
  Lay calmly buried on that magic plain.
And he who wander'd with me in my dream,
  Told me their histories as we onward went,
Till the grave shone with such a hallow'd beam,
  Such pleasure with their memory seem'd blent
That, when we look'd to heaven, our upward
    eyes
With no funeral sadness mock'd the skies!

"Then, change of scene, and time, and place
    once more;
  And by a Gothic window, richly bright,
Whose stain'd armorial bearings on the floor
  Flung the quaint tracery of their color'd light,
We sate together: his most noble head
  Bent o'er the storied tome of other days,
And still he commented on all we read,
  And taught me what to love, and what to
    praise,
Then Spenser made the summer-day seem brief,
  Or Milton sounded with a loftier song,
Then Cowper charm'd, with lays of gentle
    grief,
  Or rough old Dryden roll'd the hour along.
Or, in his varied beauty dearer still,
Sweet Shakspeare changed the world around at
    will;
And we forgot the sunshine of that room

To sit with Jacquez in the forest gloom;
To look abroad with Juliet's anxious eye
For her boy-lover 'neath the moonlight sky;
Stand with Macbeth upon the haunted heath
Or weep for gentle Desdemona's death;
Watch, on bright Cydnus' wave, the glittering
sheen
And silken sails of Egypt's wanton queen;
Or roam with Ariel through that island strange
Where spirits, and not men, were wont to range,
Still struggling on through brake, and bush, and
hollow,
Hearing that sweet voice calling—'Follow!
follow!'

"Nor were there wanting lays of other lands,
For these were all familiar in his hands:
And Dante's dream of horror work'd its spell,—
And Petrarch's sadness on our bosom fell,—
And prison'd Tasso's—he, the coldly-loved,
The madly-loving! he, so deeply proved
By many a year of darkness, like the grave,
For her who dared not plead, or would not save,
For her who thought the poet's suit brought
shame,
Whose passion hath immortalized her name!
And Egmont, with his noble heart betray'd,—
And Carlos, haunted by a murder'd shade,—
And Faust's strange legend, sweet and wond-
'rous wild,
Stole many a tear:—Creation's loveliest child
Guileless, ensnared, and tempted Margaret,

Who could peruse thy fate with eyes unwet?
"Then, through the lands we read of, far away,
The vision led me all a summer's day:
And we look'd round on southern Italy,
Where her dark head the graceful cypress rears
In arrowy straightness and soft majesty,
And the sun's face a mellower glory wears;
Bringing, where'er his warm light richly shines,
Sweet odors from the gum-distilling pines;
And casting o'er white palaces a glow,
Like morning's hue on mountain-peaks of snow.

"Those palaces! how fair their columns rose!
Their courts, cool fountains, and wide porticos!
And ballustraded roofs, whose very form
Told what an unknown stranger was the storm!
In one of these we dwelt: its painted walls
A master's hand had been employed to trace;
Its long cool range of shadowy marble halls
Was fill'd with statues of most living grace;
While on its ceiling roll'd the fiery car
Of the bright day-god, chasing night afar,—
Or Jove's young favorite, toward Olympus' height
Soar'd with the Eagle's dark majestic flight,—
Or fair Apollo's harp seem'd freshly strung,
All heaven group'd round him, listening while he sung.

"So, in the garden's plann'd and planted bound
All wore the aspect of enchanted ground ;
Thick orange-groves, close arching over head,
Shelter'd the paths our footsteps loved to tread;
Or ilex-trees shut out, with shadow sweet,
Th' oppressive splendor of the noontide heat.
Through the bright vista, at each varying turn
Gleam'd the white statue, or the graceful urn ;
And, paved with many a curved and twisted line
Of fair Mosaic's strange and quaint design,
Terrace on terrace rose, with steep so slight,
That scarce the pausing eye inquired the height,
Till stretch'd beneath in far perspective lay
The glittering city and the deep blue bay!
Then as we turn'd again to groves and bowers,
(Rich with the perfume of a thousand flowers,)
The sultry day was cheated of its force
By the sweet winding of some streamlet's course:
From sculptured arch, and ornamented walls,
Rippled a thousand tiny waterfalls,
While here and there an open basin gave
Rest to the eye and freshness to the wave ;
Here, high above the imprison'd waters, stood
Some imaged Naiad, guardian of the flood;
There, in a cool and grotto-like repose,
The sea-born goddess from her shell arose ;
Or river-god his fertile urn display'd,
Gushing at distance through the long arcade,—
Or Triton, lifting his wild conch on high,
Spouted his silver tribute to the sky,

Or, lovelier still, (because to Nature true,
Even in the thought creative genius drew,)
Some statue-nymph, her bath of beauty o'er,
Stood gently bending by the rocky shore,
And, like Bologna's sweet and graceful dream,
From her moist hair wrung out the living stream.

"Bright was the spot! and still we linger'd on
Unwearied, till the summer-day was done;
Till He, who, when the morning dew was wet,
In glory rose—in equal glory set.
Fair sank his light, unclouded to the last,
And o'er that land its glow of beauty cast;
And the sweet breath of evening air went forth
To cool the bosom of the fainting earth;
To bid the pale-leaved olives lightly wave
Upon their seaward slope (whose waters lave
With listless gentleness the golden strand,
And scarcely leave, and scarce return to land;)
Or with its wings of freshness, wandering round
Visit the heights of many a villa crown'd,
Where the still pine and cypress, side by side.
Look from their distant hills on Ocean's tide.

"The cypress and the pine! Ah, still I see
These thy green children, lovely Italy!
Nature's dear favorites, allow'd to wear
Their summer hue throughout the circling year
And oft, when wandering out at even-time
To watch the sunsets of a colder clime,
As the dim landscape fades and grows more faint

Fancy's sweet power a different scene shall
paint;
Enrich with deeper tints the colors given
To the pale beauty of our English heaven,—
Bid purple mountains rise among the clouds,
Or deem their mass some marble palace
shrouds,—
Trace on the red horizon's level line,
In outlines dark, the high majestic pine,—
And hear, amid the groups of English trees,
His sister cypress murmuring to the breeze!

"Never again shall evening, sweet and still,
Gleam upon river, mountain, rock, or hill,—
Never again shall fresh and budding spring,
Or brighter summer, hue of beauty bring,
In this, the clime where 'tis my lot to dwell,
But shall recall, as by a magic spell,
Thy scenes, dear land of poetry and song!
Bid thy fair statues on my memory throng;
Thy glorious pictures gleam upon my sight
Like fleeting shadows o'er the summer light
And send my haunted heart to dwell once more,
Glad and entranced by thy delightful shore—
Thy shore, where rolls that blue and tideless sea,
Bright as thyself, thou radiant Italy!

"And there (where Beauty's spirit sure had
birth,
Though she hath wander'd since upon the
earth,
And scatter'd, as she pass'd, some sparks of
thought,

Such as of old her sons of genius wrought,
To show what strength the immortal soul can wield
E'en here, in this its dark and narrow field,
And fills us with a fond inquiring thirst
To see that land which claim'd her triumphs first)
Music was brought—with soft impressive power—
To fill with varying joy the varying hour.
We welcomed it; for welcome still to all
It comes, in cottage, court, or lordly hall;
And in the long bright summer evenings, oft
We sate and listened to some measure soft
From many instruments; or, faint and lone,
(Touch'd by his gentle hand, or by my own,)
The little lute its chorded notes would send
Tender and clear; and with our voices blend
Cadence so true, that, when the breeze swept by,
One mingled echo floated on its sigh!

"And still as day by day we saw depart,
I was the living idol of his heart:
How to make joy a portion of the air
That breathed around me, seem'd his only care.
For me the harp was strung, the page was turn'd;
For me the morning rose, the sunset burn'd;
For me the Spring put out her verdant suit;
For me the Summer flower, the Autumn fruit,
The very world seem'd mine, so mighty strove
For my contentment, that enduring love.

"I see him still, dear mother! Still I hear
That voice so deeply soft, so strangely clear;
Still in the air wild wandering echoes float,
And bring my dream's sweet music note for note!
Oh! shall those sounds no more my fancy bless,
Which fill my heart and on my memory press?
Shall I no more those sunset clouds behold,
Floating like bright transparent thrones of gold?
The skies, the seas, the hills of glorious blue;
The glades and groves, with glories shining through;
The bands of red and purple, richly seen
Athwart the sky of pale, faint, gem-like green;
When the breeze slept, the earth lay hush'd and still,
When the low sun sank slanting from the hill,
And slow and amber-tinged the moon uprose,
To watch his farewell hour in glory close?
Is all that radiance past—gone by forever—
And must there in its stead forever be
The gray, sad sky, the cold and clouded river,
And dismal dwellings by the wintry sea?
E'er half a summer, altering day by day,
In fickle brightness, here, hath pass'd away!
And was that form (whose love might still sustain)
Naught but a vapor of the dreaming brain?
Would I had slept for ever!"
Sad she sigh'd;
To whom the mournful mother thus replied:—

"Upbraid not Heaven, whose wisdom thus would rule

A world whose changes are the soul's bes
school:
All dream like thee, and 'tis for Mercy's sake
That those who dream the wildest, soonest
wake;
All deem Perfection's system would be found
In giving earthly sense no stint or bound;
All look for happiness beneath the sun,
And each expects what God hath given to *none*.

"In what an idle luxury of joy
Would thy spoil'd heart its useless hours em-
ploy!
In what a selfish loneliness of light
Wouldst thou exist, read we thy dream aright
How hath thy sleeping spirit broke the chain
Which knits thy human lot to other's pain,
And made this world of peopled millions seem
For thee and for the lover of thy dream!

"Think not my heart with cold indifference
heard
The various feelings which in thine have stirr'd,
Or that its sad and weary currents know
Faint sympathy, except for human woe:
Well have the dormant echoes of my breast
Answer'd the joys thy gentle voice express'd;
Conjured a vision of the stately mate
With whom the flattering vision link'd thy fate;
And follow'd thee through grove and woodland
wild,

Where so much natural beauty round thee smiled.

"What man so worldly-wise, or chill'd by age,
Who, bending o'er the faint descriptive page,
Recalls not such a scene in some far nook—
(Whereon his eyes, perchance, no more shall look;)
Some hawthorn copse, some gnarl'd majestic tree,
The favorite play-place of his infancy?
Who has not felt for Cowper's sweet lament,
When twelve years' course their cruel change had sent;
When his fell'd poplars gave no further shade,
And low on earth the blackbird's nest was laid;
When in a desert sunshine, bare and blank,
Lay the green field and river's mossy bank;
And melody of bird or branch no more
Rose with the breeze that swept along the shore?

"Few are the hearts, (nor theirs of kindliest frame,)
On whom fair Nature holds not such a claim;
And oft, in after-life, some simple thing—
A bank of primroses in early spring—
The tender scent which hidden violets yield—
The sight of cowslips in a meadow-field—
Or young laburnum's pendant yellow chain
May bring the favorite play-place back again

Our youthful mates are gone; some dead, some
changed,
With whom that pleasant spot was gladly ranged;
Ourselves, perhaps, more alter'd e'en than
they—
But *there* still blooms the blossom-showering
May;
There still along the hedge-row's verdant line
The linnet sings, the thorny brambles twine;
Still in the copse a troop of merry elves
Shout—the gay image of our former selves;
And still, with sparkling eyes and eager hands
Some rosy urchin high on tiptoe stands,
And plucks the ripest berries from the bough—
Which tempts a different generation now!

"What though no *real* beauty haunt that spot.
By graver minds beheld and noticed not?
Can we forget that once to our young eyes
It wore the aspect of a Paradise?
No; still around its hallow'd precinct lives
The fond mysterious charm that memory gives,
The man recalls the feelings of the boy,
And clothes the meanest flower with freshness
and with joy.

"Nor think by elder hearts forgotten quite
Love's whisper'd words; youth's sweet and
strange delight;
They live—though after-memories fade away;
They live to cheer life's slow declining day;

Haunting the widow by her lonely hearth,
As, meekly smiling at her children's mirth,
She spreads her fair thin hands toward the fire,
To seek the warmth their slacken'd veins require:
O' gladdening her to whom Heaven's mercy spares
Her old companion with his silver hairs;
And while he dozes—changed, and dull, and weak—
And his hush'd grandchild signs, but dares not speak,—
Bidding her watch, with many a tender smile,
The wither'd form which slumbers all the while

"Yes! sweet the voice of those we loved! the tone
Which cheers our memory as we sit alone,
And will not leave us; the o'er-mastering force,
Whose under-current's strange and hidden course
Bids some chance word, by colder hearts forgot,
Return—and still return—yet weary not
The ear which wooes its sameness! How, when Death
Hath stopp,d with ruthless hands some precious breath,
The memory of the voice he hath destroy'd
Lives in our souls, as in an aching void!
How, through the varying fate of after-years,
When stifled sorrow weeps but casual tears,
If some stray tone seem *like* the voice we know

The heart leaps up with answer faint and true!
Greeting again that sweet, long-vanish'd sound,
As, in earth's nooks of ever-haunted ground,
Strange accident, or man's capricious will,
Wakes the lone echoes, and they answer still!

"Oh! what a shallow fable cheats the age,
When the lost lover, on the motley stage,
Wrapp'd from his mistress in some quaint disguise,
Deceives her ears, because he cheats her eyes!
Rather, if all could fade which charm'd us first,—
If, by some magic stroke, some plague-spot cursed,
All outward semblance left the form beloved
A wreck unrecognised, and half disproved,
At the dear sound of that familiar voice
Her waken'd heart should tremble and rejoice,
Leap to its faith at once,—and spurn the doubt
Which, on such showing, barr'd his welcome out!

"And if even *words* are sweet, what, what is song,
When lips we love, the melody prolong?
How thrills the soul, and vibrates to that lay,
Swells with the glorious sound, or dies away!
How, to the cadence of the simplest words
That ever hung upon the wild harp's chords,
The breathless heart lies listening; as it felt
All life within it on that music dwelt.

And hush'd the beating pulse's rapid power
By its own will, for that enchanted hour!

"Ay! *then* to those who love the science well,
Music becomes a passion and a spell!
Music, the tender child of rudest times,
The gentle native of all lands and climes;
Who hymns alike man's cradle and his grave,
Lulls the low cot, or peals along the nave;
Cheers the poor peasant, who his native hills
With wild Tyrolean echoes sweetly fills;
Inspires the Indian's low monotonous chant,
Weaves skilful melodies, for Luxury's haunt;
And still, through all these changes, lives the
same,
Spirit without a home, without a name,
Coming, where all is discord, strife, and sin,
To prove some innate harmony within
Our listening souls; and lull the heaving breast
With the dim vision of an unknown rest!

"But, dearest child, though many a joy be
given
By the pure bounty of all-pitying Heaven,—
Though sweet emotions in our hearts have birth,
As flowers are spangled on the lap of earth,—
Though, with the flag of Hope and Triumph
hung
High o'er our heads, we start when life is young,
And onward cheer'd, by sense, and sight, and
sound,

Like a launch'd bark, we enter with a bound;
Yet must the dark cloud lour, the tempest fall,
And the same chance of shipwreck waits for all.
Happy are they who leave the harboring land
Not for a summer voyage, hand in hand,
Pleasure's light slaves: but with an earnest eye
Exploring all the future of their sky;
That so, when Life's career at length is past,
To the right haven they may steer at last,
And safe from hidden rock, or open gale,
Lay by the oar, and furl the slacken'd sail,—
To anchor deeply on that tranquil shore
Where vexing storms can never reach them
more!

"Wouldst thou be singled out by partial
Heaven
The ONE to whom a cloudless lot is given?
Look round the world, and see what fate is there,
Which justice can pronounce exempt from care:
Though bright they bloom to empty outward show
There lurks in each some canker-worm of woe;
Still by some thorn the onward step is cross'd,
Nor least repining those who 're envied most:
The poor have struggling, toil, and wounded
pride,
Which seeks, and seeks in vain, its rags to hide;
The rich, cold jealousies, intrigues, and strife,
And heart-sick discontent which poisons life;
The loved are parted by the hand of Death
The hated live to curse each other's breath:
The wealthy noble mourns the want of heirs

While, each the object of incessant prayers,
Gay, hardy sons, around the widow's board,
With careless smiles devour her scanty hoard;
And hear no sorrow in her stifled sigh,
And see no terror in her anxious eye,—
While *she* in fancy antedates the time
When, scatter'd far and wide in many a clime,
These heirs to nothing but their Father's name
Must earn their bread, and struggle hard for fame;
To sultry India sends her fair-hair'd boy—
Sees the dead desk another's youth employ—
And parts with one to sail the uncertain main,
Never perhaps on earth to meet again!

"Nor e'en does Love, whose fresh and radiant beam
Gave added brightness to thy wandering dream,
Preserve from bitter touch of ills unknown,
But rather brings strange sorrows of its own.
Various the ways in which our souls are tried;
Love often fails where most our faith relied;
Some wayward heart may win, without a thought,
That which thine own by sacrifice hath bought;
May carelessly aside the treasure cast,
And yet be madly worshipp'd to the last;
Whilst thou, forsaken, grieving, left to pine-
Vainly may'st claim his plighted faith as thine;
Vainly his idol's charms with thine compare,
And know thyself as young, as bright, as fair'
Vainly in jealous pangs consume thy day,

And waste the sleepless night in tears away
Vainly with forced indulgence strive to smile
In the cold world, heart-broken all the while,
Or from its glittering and unquiet crowd,
Thy brain on fire, thy spirit crush'd and bow'd,
Creep home unnoticed, there to weep alone,
Mock'd by a claim which gives thee not thine own,
Which leaves thee bound through all thy blighted youth
To him whose perjured soul hath broke its truth;
While the just world, beholding thee bereft,
Scorns—not his sin—but *thee*, for being left!

"Ah! never to the Sensualist appeal,
Nor deem his frozen bosom aught can feel.
Affection, root of all fond memories,
Which bids what once hath charm'd for ever please,
He knows not: all thy beauty could inspire
Was but a sentiment of low desire:
If from thy cheek the rose's hue be gone,
How should love stay which loved for that alone?
Or, if thy youthful face be still as bright
As when it first entranced his eager sight,
Thou art *the same;* there is thy fault, thy crime,
Which fades the charms yet spared by rapid Time,
Talk to him of the happy days gone by,
Conceal'd aversion chills his shrinking eye:
While in thine agony thou still dost rave,
Impatient wishes doom thee to the grave;

And if his cold and selfish thought had power
T' accelerate the fatal final hour,
The silent murder were already done,
And thy white tomb would glitter in the sun.
What wouldst thou hold by? What is it to him
That for his sake thy weeping eyes are dim?
His pall'd and weary senses rove apart,
And for his heart—thou never *hadst* his heart.

"True, there is better love, whose balance just
Mingles Soul's instinct with our grosser dust,
And leaves affection, strengthening day by day,
Firm to assault, impervious to decay.
To such, a star of hope thy love shall be
Whose steadfast light he still desires to see;
And age shall vainly mar thy beauty's grace,
Or wantons plot to steal into thy place,
Or wild Temptation, from her hidden bowers,
Fling o'er his path her bright but poisonous flowers,—
Dearer to him than all who thus beguile,
Thy faded face, and thy familiar smile;
Thy glance, which still hath welcomed him for years,
Now bright with gladness, and now dim with tears!
And if (for we are weak) division come
On wings of discord to that happy home,
Soon is the painful hour of anger past,
Too sharp, too strange an agony to last;
And, like some river's bright abundant tide

Which art or accident hath forced aside,
The well-springs of affection, gushing o'er,
Back to their natural channels flow once more

"Ah! sad it is when one thus link'd departs
When Death, that mighty severer of true hearts,
Sweeps through the halls so lately loud in mirth,
And leaves pale Sorrow weeping by the hearth.
Bitter it is to wander there alone,
To fill the vacant place, the empty chair,
With a dear vision of the loved one gone,
And start to see it vaguely melt in air!
Bitter to find all joy that once hath been
Double its value when 'tis pass'd away,—
To feel the blow which Time should make less keen
Increase its burden each successive day,—
To need good counsel, and to miss the voice,
The ever trusted, and the ever true,
Whose tones were wont to cheer our faltering choice,
And show what holy Virtue bade us do,—
To bear deep wrong and bow the widow'd head
In helpless anguish, no one to defend;
Or worse,—in lieu of him, the kindly dead,
Claim faint assistance from some lukewarm friend—
Yet scarce perceive the extent of all our loss
Till the fresh tomb be green with gathering moss—
Till many a morn have met our sadden'd eyes,
With none to say "Good morrow;"—many an eve

Send its red glory through the tranquil skies,
Each bringing with it deeper cause to grieve!

"This is a destiny which may be thine—
The common grief: God will'd it should be mine:
Short was the course our happy love had run,
And hard it was to say 'Thy will be done!'

"Yet those whom man, not God, hath parted, know
A heavier pang, a more enduring woe;
No softening memory mingles with *their* tears,
Still the wound rankles on through dreary years,
Still the heart feels, in bitterest hours of blame,
It dares not curse the long-familiar name;
Still, vainly free, through many a cheerless day,
From weaker ties turn helplessly away,
Sick for the smiles that bless'd its home of yore,
The natural joys of life that come no more;
And, all bewilder'd by the abyss, whose gloom
Dark and impassable as is the tomb,
Lies stretch'd between the future and the past,—
Sinks into deep and cold despair at last.

"Heaven give thee poverty, disease, or death,
Each varied ill that waits on human breath,
Rather than bid thee linger out thy life
In the long toil of such unnatural strife.
To wander through the world unreconciled,

Heart weary as a spirit-broken child,
And think it were an hour of bliss like heaven
If thou could'st *die*—forgiving and forgiven,—
Or with a feverish hope of anguish born,
(Nerving thy mind to feel indignant scorn
Of all the cruel foes who 'twixt ye stand,
Holding thy heartstrings with a reckless hand,)
Steal to his presence, now unseen so long,
And claim *his* mercy who hath dealt the wrong!
Into the aching depths of thy poor heart
  Dive, as it were, even to the roots of pain,
And wrench up thoughts that tear thy soul apart,
  And burn like fire through thy bewilder'd brain.
Clothe them in passionate words of wild appeal
To teach thy fellow-creature *how* to feel,—
Pray, weep, exhaust thyself in maddening tears,—
Recall the hopes, the influences of years,—
Kneel, dash thyself upon the senseless ground,
Writhe as the worm writhes with dividing wound,—
Invoke the heaven that knows thy sorrow's truth,
By all the softening memories of youth—
By every hope that cheer'd thine earlier day—
By every tear that washes wrath away—
By every old remembrance long gone by—
By every pang that makes thee yearn to die;
And learn at length how deep and stern a blow
Near hands can strike, and yet no pity show!

"Oh! weak to suffer, savage to inflict,
  Is man's commingling nature; hear him now

Some transient trial of his life depict,
Hear him in holy rites a suppliant bow;
See him shrink back from sickness and from pain,
And in his sorrow to his God complain;
'Remit my trespass, spare my sin,' he cries,
'All-merciful, Almighty, and All-wise;
Quench this affliction's bitter whelming tide,
Draw out thy barbed arrow from my side:'—
—And rises from that mockery of prayer
To hale some brother-debtor to despair!

"May this be spared thee! Yet be sure, my child,
(Howe'er that dream thy fancy hath beguiled,)
Some sorrow lurks to cloud thy future fate;
Thy share of tears,—come early or come late,—
Must still be shed; and 'twere as vain a thing
To ask of Nature one perpetual spring
As to evade those sad autumnal hours,
Or deem thy path of life should bloom, all flowers."

She ceased: and that fair maiden heard the truth
With the fond passionate despair of youth,
Which, new to suffering, gives its sorrow vent
In outward signs and bursts of wild lament:-

"If this be so, then, mother, let me die
Ere yet the glow hath faded from my sky!
Let me die young; before the holy trust

In human kindness crumbles into dust;
Before I suffer what I have not earn'd,
Or see by treachery my truth return'd;
Before the love I live for, fades away;
Before the hopes I cherish'd most, decay;
Before the withering touch of fearful change
Makes some familiar face look cold and strange,
Or some dear heart, close knitted to my own,
By perishing, hath left me more alone!
Though death be bitter, I can brave its pain
Better than all which threats if I remain:
While my soul, freed from ev'ry chance of ill,
Soars to that God whose high mysterious will
Sent me, foredoom'd to grief, with wandering feet,
To group my way through all this fair deceit!"

Her parent heard the words with grieved amaze,
And thus return'd, with calm reproving gaze:—

'Blaspheme not Heaven with rash impatient speech,
Nor deem, at thine own hour, its rest to reach,
Unhappy child! The full appointed time
Is His to choose; and when the sullen chime,
And deep-toned striking of the funeral bell,
Thy fate to earthly ears shall sadly tell,
Oh! may the death thou talk'st of as a boon,
Find thee prepared,—nor come even then too soon!

"True, ere thou meet'st that long and dreamless sleep,
Thy heart must ache—thy weary eyes must weep:
It is our human lot! The fariest child
That e'er on loving mother brightly smiled,—
Most watch'd, most tended—ere his eyelids close,
Hath had his little share of infant woes,
And dies familiar with the sense of grief,
Though for all else his life hath been too brief!
But shall we therefore, murmuring against God,
Question the justice of his chastening rod,
And look to earthly joys as though *they* were
The prize immortal souls were given to share?
"Oh! were such joys and this vain world alone
The term of human hope—where, where would be
The victims of some tyranny unknown,
Who sank, still conscious that the *mind* was free?
They that have lain in dungeons years on years,
No voice to cheer their darkness,—they whose pain
Of horrid torture wrung forth blood with tears,
Murder'd, perhaps, for some rapacious gain,—
They who have stood, bound to the martyr's stake,
While the sharp flames ate through the blistering skin,—
They that have bled for some high cause's sake,—

They that have perish'd for another's sin,
And from the scaffold to that God appeal'd
To whom the naked heart is all reveal'd,
Against the shortening of life's narrow span
By the blind rage and false decree of man?
And where obscurer sufferers—they who slept
And left no name on history's random page,
But in God's book of reckoning, sternly kept,
Live on from year to year, from age to age?
The poor—the laboring poor! whose weary lives,
Through many a freezing night and hungry day,
Are a reproach to him who only strives
In luxury to waste his hours away,—
The patient poor! whose insufficient means
Make sickness dreadful, yet by whose low bed
Oft in meek prayers some fellow sufferer leans,
And trusts in Heaven while destitute of bread;
The workhouse orphan, left without a friend;
Or weak forsaken child of want and sin,
Whose helpless life begins, as it must end,
By men disputing who shall take it in;
Who clothe, who aid that spark to linger here,
Which for mysterious purpose God hath given
To struggle through a day of toil and fear,
And meet him—with the proudest—up in heaven!
These were, and are not:—shall we therefore deem
That they have vanish'd like a sleeper's dream?

Or that one half creation is to know
Luxurious joy, and others only woe,
And so go down into the common tomb,
With none to question their unequal doom?
Shall we give credit to a thought so fond?
Ah! no—the world beyond—the world beyond.
There, shall the desolate heart regain its own.
There, the oppress'd shall stand before God's
throne!
There, when the tangled web is all explain'd,
Wrong suffer'd, pain inflicted, grief disdain'd,
Man's proud mistaken judgments and false scorn
Shall melt like mists before uprising morn,
And holy truth stand forth serenely bright,
In the rich flood of God's eternal light!

"Then shall the Lazarus of the earth have
rest—
The rich man judgment—and the grieving
breast
Deep peace for ever. Therefore look thou not
So much to what on earth shall be thy lot,
As to thy fate hereafter,—to that day
When like a scroll this world shall pass away,
And what thou here hast done, or here enjoy'd,
Import but to thy *soul*:—all else destroy'd!

"And have thou faith in human nature still;
Though evil thoughts abound, and acts of ill;
Though innocence in sorrow shrouded be,
And tyranny's strong step walk bold and free.
For many a kindly generous deed is done

Which leaves no record underneath the sun—
Self-abnegating love and humble worth,
Which yet shall consecrate our sinful earth!
He that deals blame, and yet forgets to praise,
Who sets brief storms against long summer-days,
Hath a sick judgment. Shall the usual joy
Be all forgot, and nought our minds employ,
Through the long course of ever-varing years,
But temporary pain and casual tears?
And shall we *all* condemn, and *all* distrust,
Because some men are false and some unjust?
Forbid it heaven! far better 'twere to be
Dupe of the fond impossibility
Of light and radiance which thy vision gave,
Than thus to live Suspicion's bitter slave.
Give credit to thy mortal brother's heart
For all the good than in thine own hath part,
And, cheerfully as honest prudence may,
Trust to his proffer'd hand's protecting stay:
For God, who made this teeming earth so full,
And made the proud dependent on the dull—
The strong upon the weak—thereby would show
One common bond should link us all below.

"And visit not with a severer scorn
Faults, whose deep root was with our nature born,
From which—though others woo'd thee just as vain—
Thou, differently tempted, didst abstain:
Nor dwell on points of creed—assuming right
To judge how holy in his Maker's sight

Is he who at a different altar bends ;
For hence have ris'n the bitterest feuds of
friends,
The wildest wars of nations ; age on age
Hath desecrated thus dark History's page ;
And still (though not, perhaps, with fire and
sword)
Reckless we raise ' The banner of the Lord !'
Mock Heaven's calm mercy by the plea we
make,
That all is done for gentle Jesus' sake,—
Disturb the consciences of weaker men,—
Employ the scholar's art, the bigot's pen,—
And rouse the wrathful and the spirit-proud
To language bitter, vehement, and loud,
Whose unconvincing fury wounds the ear,
And seeking, with some sharp and haughty
sneer,
How best the opposing party may be stung,—
Pleads for religion with a devil's tongue !

" Oh ! shall God tolerate the meanest prayer
That humbly seeks his high supernal throne,
And man—presumptuous Pharisee—declare
His fellow's voice less welcome than his own ?
Is it a theme for wild and warring words
How best to satisfy the Maker's claim ?
In rendering to the Lord what is the Lord's,
Doth not the thought of violence bring shame ?
Think ye he gave the branching forest tree
To furnish fagots for the funeral pyre ?
Or bid his sunrise light the world, to see

Pale tortured victims perish there by fire?
No! oft on earth, dragg'd forth in pain to die,
The heretic may groan—the martyr bleed—
But, set before his Sovereign Judge on high,
'Tis man's *offence* condemns him, not his creed.
His first commandment was to worship Him;
His next—to love the creature He hath made:
How blind the eyes of those who read, how dim,
Who see not here religious fury stay'd!
From the proud *half*-fulfilment of his law
Sternly he turns away his awful face,
Nor will contentment from their service draw,
Who fail to grant a fellow-creature grace.
Haply the days of martyrdom are past,
But still we see, without a visible end,
The bitter warfare of opinion last,
Tho' God hath will'd that man should be man's friend.
Therefore do thou, e'er yet thy youthful heart
Be tinged with their revilings, safe retreat,
And in those fierce discussions bear no part,—
Odius in all—in woman most unmeet,—
But in the still dark night, and rising day,
Humbly collect thy thoughts, and humbly pray.

"And be not thou cast down, because thy lot
The glory of thy dream resembleth not.
Not for herself was woman first create,
Nor yet to be man's idol, but his mate.
Still from his birth his cradled bed she tends,
The first, the last, the faithfulest of friends;

Still finds her place in sickness or in woe,
Humble to comfort, strong to undergo;
Still in the depth of weeping sorrow tries
To watch his death-bed with her patient eyes!
And doubt not thou,—(although at times deceived,
Outraged, insulted, slander'd, crush'd, and grieved;
Too often made a victim or a toy,
With years of sorrow for an hour of joy;
Too oft forgot midst Pleasure's circling wiles,
Or only valued for her rosy smiles,—)
That in the frank and generous heart of man,
The place she holds accords with Heaven's high plan;
Still, if from wandering sin reclaim'd at all,
He sees in *her* the angel of recall;
Still, in the sad and serious hours of life,
Turns to the sister, mother, friend or wife;
Views with a heart of fond and trustful pride
His faithful partner by his calm fireside;
And oft, when barr'd of Fortune's fickle grace,
Blank ruin stares him darkly in the face,
Leans his faint head upon her kindly breast,
And owns her power to soothe him into rest,-
Owns what the gift of woman's love is worth
To cheer his toils and trials upon earth!

" Sure it is much, this delegated power
To be consoler of man's heaviest hour!
The guardian angel of a life of care,
Allow'd to stand 'twixt him and his despair!

Such service may be made a holy task;
And more, 'twere vain to hope, and rash to ask,
Therefore, oh! loved and lovely, be content,
And take thy lot, with joy and sorrow blent.
Judge none; yet let thy share of conduct be,
As knowing judgment shall be pass'd on thee
Here and hereafter; so, still undismay'd,
And guarded by thy sweet thoughts' tranquil shade,
Undazzled by the changeful rays which threw
Their light across thy path while life was new,
Thou shalt move sober on,—expecting less,
Therefore the more enjoying, happiness."

There was a pause; then, with a tremulous smile,
The maiden turn'd and press'd her mother's hand:—
"Shall I not bear what thou hast borne e'rewhile?
Shall I, rebellious, Heaven's high will withstand?
No! cheerly on, my wandering path I'll take,
Nor fear the destiny I did not make:
Though earthly joy grow dim—though pleasure waneth—
This thou hast taught thy child, that GOD remaineth!"

And from her mother's fond protecting side
She went into the world a youthful bride.

www.ingramcontent.com/pod-product-compliance
Lightning Source LLC
LaVergne TN
LVHW020234110826
845151LV00003B/924

* 9 7 8 1 4 2 5 5 3 0 4 2 6 *